SINGIN'

The story of a No   ly

1859 - 1965

Glanton House from village circa 1910

Joyce Robertson

GHG

Edited from the original manuscript
by
The Glanton Heritage Group

MMXIII

First published 2013
by
Bailiffgate Publishing
in association with
Carnegie Book Production

ISBN No. 978-0-9926836-0-3

Printed and bound by Short Run Press Limited, Exeter

Typeset in Caslon Openface : Caslon : Futura : Intimacy

Mr M Cully kindly grants permission to Glanton Heritage Group
to publish the Robertson photographic images used within
Singin' Hinnies.

TO
THE MEMORY OF MY FATHER
WILL

NOTE FOR NON-NORTHUMBRIANS

'Singin' hinnies' are Northumbrian girdle cakes. As 'hinny' is also a term of endearment for Northumbrian children, the title seemed appropriate to the story of this happy family.

Joyce Robertson
1975

This book has been laid out following Joyce's manuscript as closely as possible. The dialect, spelling, grammar and punctuation are hers

GHG

 Singin' Hinnies recipe page 180

FOREWORD

The first part of this book is based largely on the voluminous correspondence, which passed between the various members of the family, and which, bless them, they hoarded for the rest of their lives. The second part, while relying to some extent on letters, has been compiled mainly from my own vivid recollections of my early days at Glanton.

My thanks are due to the Librarian of the Royal College of Physicians, the Archivist of Edinburgh Royal Infirmary and the Librarian of Charing Cross Hospital for information regarding my father and grandfather's student careers. I am grateful to Sir Alec Douglas-Home, K.T., M.P. for permission to include the incident recorded on page 126. For information regarding my grandmother's financial affairs I am indebted to R.F. Walker, Esq., M.A., LL.M., whose firm have undertaken my family's legal business through three generations. I am also grateful to the late Duchess of Grafton, the Rev. J. Meakle of Alnwick, the Rev. W.A. Rodgers of Wooler and others who have helped to fill in the background.

Joyce Robertson

CONTENTS

PART I

1859-1901

PART II

1902-1965

1859 – 1901

'The tale as 'twas said'
Scott: The Lay of the Last Minstrel

PROLOGUE

'Prithee, pretty maiden, will you marry me?'
W.S. Gilbert: Patience

It was a mild March afternoon in the year 1859. There was a hint of spring in the air, and Dr. William Robertson was taking a stroll in his garden at Glanton House, where he had been in practice for the last eleven years. The Northumbrian countryside, emerging at last from the grip of its long winter, was palely green in the early spring sunshine, and William was enjoying the sweet smell of new grass and the distant view of the Cheviot Hills. But he was lonely. Though in his late thirties, he was still a bachelor, and Glanton House was over-large for a single man.

He glanced casually over the fence to the garden of the house next door – a late seventeenth century house incongruously known as 'The Villa' – his thoughts far away. Suddenly he stopped. Coming down the path, her crinoline swaying to her graceful walk, a shawl draped around her shoulders, was a tall slender girl. She had grey eyes and light brown hair demurely parted in the middle and draped low over her cheeks in the current fashion. She was very comely, and very young. William knew that his neighbours had engaged a governess, but he had expected her to be a prim middle-aged woman, and had taken little interest. Surely this enchanting child could not be the governess?

William bowed, and with a shy smile she returned his greeting. In that moment William, the confirmed bachelor, fell headlong in love.

Yes, she told him, she <u>was</u> the governess; her name was Elizabeth White and she lived at Shotley Bridge, near Durham. She was only nineteen, and had never been so far from home. She, too, was lonely.

After that day they had many conversations over the garden fence. Then one summer's evening, greatly daring, William asked Elizabeth to take a walk with him. They left the village by the Playwell Lane and, after a mile or so, turned off the road to climb a steep little path on the way to Titlington Mount. There, while they paused to rest on a stile, William asked Elizabeth to marry him. She accepted, they were married at Bishop Wearmouth the following year, and Elizabeth moved into Glanton House.

William and Elizabeth were to become my grandparents.

CHAPTER I

ANCESTORS

'Our ancestors are very good kind of folks'
Sheridan: The Rivals

Elizabeth White

Queen Victoria had been on the throne only two years when Elizabeth was born on 8th July 1839. She came of an old Durham family, and her father, Thomas White, was a surgeon at Shotley Bridge. He was one of a long line of Thomas Whites, for it was apparently a tradition in the family that the eldest son in each generation should be named Thomas*. The earliest of which we have any record was born in the latter half of the seventeenth century, and lived at Shincliffe, a few miles from Durham. His great-grandson, Thomas, married Ann Harrison in 1798, and she bore him sixteen children. Their names, with dates – even exact hours – of birth were inscribed in white paint on a scroll of pale green silk, which still exists. The eldest of this brood married Margaret Lamb and became the father of eight children, one of whom was my grandmother, Elizabeth, but of this large family only three survived childhood. Elizabeth's elder brother (Thomas, of course) died without

---

*   *In the archives of Bristol there are no less than three Thomas Whites who figure prominently in the Corporation records in the 16th and 17th centuries – Mr Dr and Sir Thomas (the last an alderman of the City of London). One wonders whether they were connected with the Whites of Durham.*

issue, so, after many generations, the old tradition of nomenclature lapsed. Her younger brother, Conrad, was to make a considerable impact on the lives of her children.

In the late 1850s Elizabeth's father died, leaving the family in straightened circumstances, and it became necessary for his young daughter to seek some form of lucrative employment. With no training and no qualifications other than a cultured background, a lively intelligence and considerable charm, she took one of the few occupations open to a young Victorian gentlewoman; she became a governess. So it came about that in 1859 she said goodbye to her family, and with trepidation, lonely and sad at heart, went to live at the Villa.

William Robertson was of Highland descent. The main branch of the clan, to which he belonged, lived originally at Struan in Perthshire, being descended from King Duncan, the victim of Macbeth, by way of an irregular union on the part of the king's great-great-grandson. But the earliest ancestor of our own family of whom we have any definite knowledge is John Robertson, who was a weaver and lived at Kinross, many miles south of the homeland. In 1742 John gave half an acre of land to his son, James, who was also a weaver. James's son, another John (in this family the eldest sons were named James and John alternately), was a 'portioner of muire'*, and possibly also a shoemaker, and he too lived at Kinross. He was said to be 'wealthy for his station'. He married Ann Henderson and died in 1835, leaving two sons and a daughter, and it would seem that his children did well for themselves. James, the eldest, became a Presbyterian minister, amassed a considerable amount of money, but lived the life of a recluse and died without issue.

James – my great grandfather – was born in 1777. After entering the ministry he was 'called' first to Coldstream, then in 1802 to the Tower Hill Church in Wooler**, just across the border in Northumberland, and here he was to spend the rest of his life. He married Jane Bolton, the daughter of a well-to-do farmer, and she brought to her marriage a dowry of £2000 – quite a fortune in those days. It was as well that she did, for in the course of fourteen years she presented James with seven sons and three

---

*   *He was probably responsible for apportioning the moorland among the crofters for the digging of peat, as is still the practice in the west of Ireland.*
**   *There were no less than three Presbyterian churches in Wooler.*

Reverend James Robertson

daughters, a large family for an impecunious minister to support, but two of the boys died in infancy. It is with James that our ancestors emerge from the shadows of the past and acquire a recognisable personality. Some of his letters survive, and we know what he looked like. An oil painting of the reverend gentleman suggests a rather stern and straight-laced cleric whom one would not care to cross. His glittering blue eyes follow one everywhere, seeming to probe into the depths of one's conscience. One can imagine him in his black gown thundering from the pulpit like a latter day John Knox. Yet there is perhaps a suggestion of kindly humour in the upward tilt of his lips, and we know that he was a very affectionate parent, and was devoted to his grandchildren.

A letter to his daughter, Ann, in 1846, when he was in his seventieth year, sheds a little light on the character of this rather autocratic gentleman:

> *'It is seldom that a letter is addressed to me now by any of my family except Edward, who I must acknowledge still recognises me as the head of my own family...... The rest write rather to one another than to me.'*

Yet, despite this rather petulant outburst, he mentions later in the same letter that 'we hear now very frequently from Eliza,' and that 'we had a letter from William by last night's post.' His daughter in law, Esther, had also written ' a few confused lines' to say that his grandson had had measles. Perhaps the trouble was that the younger generation did not address their letters to the head of the family personally. James goes on to express his thankfulness to God for sparing him and his family ' in the midst of so much distress and so many deaths around us.' In the course of nine days there had been seven deaths in Wooler. It had been a terrible winter, with several weeks of intense cold, snow and high winds. Posts had been delayed and there was a shortage of coals. 'When we sent for them they were not to be had, and even when they were eventually got, both man and horse were detained almost a whole day waiting upon them.' He envied Ann her life of plenty in Sunderland, where she had been living since her marriage to Thomas Duncan, a man of some wealth, but he exhorted her not to forget her duty to God in the midst of her 'many avocations and engagements.' He continued:

> 'I never had much delight in gossip and small talk.... They are altogether unbecoming the dignity of our reasonable nature, not to say inconsistent with our holy vocation and with our Christian prospects.'

One must respect James for his integrity and sincere faith, and he was held in great esteem during his long ministry, but one feels that life at the Manse cannot have been very gay. By this time, however, he was probably in bad health. When, in 1852, he entered on the fiftieth year of his ministry at Wooler, a jubilee dinner was held in his honour at the Black Bull Inn, when James 'in a spirit of deep and earnest piety.... stated that three years ago, in consequence of increasing infirmity, it was found necessary that a co-pastor should be obtained.' Elsewhere this co-pastor, a Mr Whyte, was referred to as 'Colleague and Successor,' and it seems probable that the dinner marked the occasion of James's retirement. His wife died in the same year, and it would appear that he was leaving the Manse, as he drew up a deed of gift making over to his three daughters certain household articles 'to prevent the same being exposed by publick sale.' To his daughters, jointly he gave all his linen, silver plate and china, a pianoforte, a tea table and two chests of drawers. As Ann was living in Sunderland, one wonders how they shared the piano and the tea table! Four months later he added 'Memoranda' making further individual bequests. To Ann he left 'the chest of drawers standing in the Back bedroom...They originally belonged to her Aunt Ann Bolton and were given to her as a present by her late Grandmother, Mrs Bolton.)* Each daughter was to have 'a Tick or feather Bed, with Bolsters and Pillows' which had belonged to their grandmother, and Eliza, the youngest, was given 'the stool or seat belonging to the Piano-forte, the cover of it having been sewed by herself...and my silver snuff-box which I received from my Congregation several years ago.' To the eldest daughter, Jane, he gave

---

*   *When she died in 1905 she left this chest of drawers to me. J.R.*

'two or three Paintings or Landscapes…having been painted by herself….
and the portrait of myself which hangs in the Dining Room here' (the oil
painting referred to above). Ann was to have 'the Purse (of gold) which
I received from my kind friends in Coldstream and its neighbourhood,
exclusive however of its valuable contents' (can we detect a flash of
humour here? Half a century had passed since James left Coldstream,
and the 'valuable contents' had no doubt been spent long ago)[*] 'together
with the gold ring that belonged to her dear Brother John – and one or
more of the Rings that belonged to and were occasionally worn by her
dear Mother'. Ann, the married woman, was the only one to receive any
jewellery. Perhaps James considered such adornments unsuitable for his
two spinster daughters. The only son to receive a gift was William, who
had the portrait of his eldest brother, John, who had died eight years
earlier.

John was outstandingly clever, and his father drove him hard. He read
the Old Testament at the age of five, and the Greek Testament when he
was seven. He, too, became a minister, was ordained in 1832, and went
to Duns, in Berwickshire. An oil painting by Mungo Burton portrays a
handsome, gentle and delicate young man, bearing little resemblance to
his stern father. A Mrs Dunn, who, as a little girl, had attended John's
church at Duns, still remembered in her old age the deep impression he
had made on her. 'He was tall and fair complexioned, with big, clear, dark
blue eyes shining with the light of the dying consumptive. He had fair,
curling hair, worn longish in the fashion of the day. He had very correct
features and a faint pink flush in his cheeks. He looked to me like an
angel from heaven, and I've never forgotten him'. He preached only of
the 'love of God to uswards,' and this impressed the little girl, because
until then all the sermons she had heard had been 'howling lectures of
Hell and Damnation and God's judgements on us Sinners'. (Perhaps she
did not hear the sermon in which he said, 'If you live and die the enemies
of the Saviour, how will you be able to endure his withering glance, and
to hear him pronounce the awful and irreversible sentence, "Depart from
me, ye cursed, into everlasting fire, prepared for the devil and his angels".
In vain will you then call upon the rocks and mountains to fall on you
and hide you from the wrath of the Lamb.')

---

[*] *James was given another purse of gold at Wooler in the fiftieth year of his ministry,
and this is in my possession – 'exclusive of its valuable contents.'*

5

In 1835 John married Esther Ainslie. His first son, James, was born in 1836, a second son, Ainslie in 1837, and a daughter, Jane (Jeannie) in the following year.

John had always been delicate. In his diary there are references to his asthma, and on a number of occasions he was prevented from taking a service owing to ill health. By September 1840, he had become so unwell that his doctor advised him to spend the winter in Jersey, and he made arrangements to go there at the end of the month. Then, in the middle of September, his younger son, Ainslie, was taken ill and died, after ten days illness, at the age of three and a half. A

Reverend John Robertson

few days later John and his wife, with their other son, James, went to St Helier, in Jersey, leaving little Jeannie at the Wooler Manse. She was a lively, lovable and happy child, and her grandparents and aunts adored her. But in February of the following year, in spite of their loving care, she contracted croup and became very ill. The doctor, in James's words, 'immediately commenced that mode of treatment which is adapted to the croup.' She was given an emetic and frequent apperients, her throat was blistered, four leeches were attached to her, and after their removal bleeding was encouraged for several hours. In spite of – or perhaps because of – this drastic treatment, Jeannie died after only three days illness, and to James fell the heart-rending task of breaking the news of this second tragedy to his son and daughter-in-law, far away in Jersey. The little girl was buried in Duns, in the same grave as the brother who had died only five months earlier.

At the beginning of April John returned to Scotland, but the six months in Jersey had done nothing to improve his health, and the following year he was obliged to resign from the ministry. He wrote two years later to his youngest sister, Eliza, who had been sent to Stirling to housekeep

6

for her uncle William, the wine merchant. He complained of fatigue, clammy feet and a disordered stomach, and suffered from breathlessness. He was, as Mrs Dunn said, dying of tuberculosis. John told Eliza of the execution that morning of a man who had murdered his brother-in-law. It was evidently carried out in public, for *'there was a great assembly of people, as usual on such occasion.'* We realised that life was not very gay for Eliza, and tried to cheer her up:

> *'You must try to occupy and amuse yourself as well as you can.'* *he wrote. 'You have a piano, I understand (though not a very good one), plenty of fancy work, some books to read, and some acquaintances to call upon...You need to feel no delicacy about accepting invitations, as you are living not in your own house, but with your Uncle, who neither gives nor receives invitations.'*

Here we have a picture of the monotonous and, to us, rather aimless life of so many Victorian girls; and the lot of the unmarried daughter was often a particularly unenviable one. Like Elizabeth White fifteen years earlier, and Elizabeth's youngest daughter, Ina, in the 1890s, Eliza had to leave her home in the prime of her youth to shoulder responsibilities in someone else's house. Unlike Elizabeth, she found no eligible bachelor living next door, and she remained unmarried.

John died later that year, at the early age of thirty-four. His only surviving child, James, was educated at Harrow and Jesus College, Cambridge. He, too, became a clergyman, but transferred his allegiance to the Church of England, eventually becoming Headmaster of Haileybury College.

James of Wooler's second son – yet another James – was a commercial traveller, and was one of the witnesses at the marriage of William and Elizabeth. The third son, Edward, was apparently in Holy Orders, the fourth was my grandfather, William, and he was followed by Alexander, who became a farmer in Roxburghshire. James's three daughters Jane, Ann and Eliza, were to play a considerable part in the lives of William's children.

James of Wooler died in 1855, in a world vastly changed from that into which he had been born. In 1777 Bonnie Prince Charlie and Dr

---

*   *The last public hanging was in 1869*

Johnson were still alive, Britain was fighting the 'rebels' in the American Colonies, the young Beethoven's music had yet to be written, and Captain Cook had but recently put the east coast of Australia on the map. One travelled on horseback or by coach along rutted highways where Jerry Abershaw and other 'gentlemen' of the road' added to the hazards of one's journey. Labourers were paid one shilling a day – if they were lucky – Beau Brummell was still unborn, and fashionable ladies taking the waters at Bath recalled nostalgically the glittering days of the late lamented Beau Nash. Before James died, Cobbett's 'Great Wen' had engulfed the villages of Kensington and Pimlico and sprawled over the fields of Surrey and Middlesex. The Industrial Revolution had changed the face of England; the Napoleonic Wars had been fought and won; the cataclysmic effects of the French Revolution had shaken the country. Gone were the stagecoach and the highwaymen; now one travelled safely on macadamised roads and railways bestraddled the country. Slavery had been abolished in the British Empire, parliament had been reformed, the first Public Health Act had been passed, income tax had become an unwelcome but accepted part of life, and the gay abandon of the eighteenth century had given place to comfortable Victorian respectability.

It is interesting to note that, while James was born in 1777, his youngest granddaughter, Ina, lived until 1965.

Tower Hill Church, Wooler, Northumberland

CHAPTER II

WILLIAM ROBERTSON M.D.

An house of ancient fame
Spenser: Prothalamion

William Robertson M.D.

William was born in 1821. He decided to break with the family tradition of going into the church, and studied medicine at Edinburgh, where he obtained his M.D. degree in 1843. Edinburgh had, at that time, one of the finest medical schools in the world. The Faculty of Medicine was founded in 1726, and three years later the first hospital came into being. The original premises, known as 'The Little House' was in Robertson's Close, off the Cowgate, and had only six beds. The salary of the Mistress (forerunner of the Matron) was £5 for the first year, and her only assistant was one servant. Ten years later the Infirmary had become sufficiently important to be granted a Royal Charter by King George II. It soon became obvious that far more accommodation was needed for the care of the sick poor, and in 1737, with a growing subscription list, the managers were able to purchase a site in what was to become known as Infirmary Street. The foundation stone for the new hospital was laid in 1738, and it was designed to accommodate eventually 228 patients. During the next hundred years it continued to grow steadily until in

1843, when William qualified, it was admitting more than 5000 patients a year.

In the previous year there had been a serious epidemic of fever (probably typhus), one of several that hit the city between 1817 and 1848. During these years various buildings had been taken over as temporary accommodation for fever patients, but even these were unable to cope with the number of cases needing hospital treatment, and the surplus had to be admitted to the Infirmary itself. In 1843 the whole hospital had to be 'cleansed' because in the previous year it had been kept so full that this task could not be carried out. One hopes that 'cleansing' referred to redecoration rather than day-to-day cleaning.

The years that William spent at the Infirmary were a time of great change and remarkable advances in surgical techniques and among the signatures on his certificate are two of the great names in surgery. One was James Young Simpson, the obstetrician and gynaecologist who, a few years later, was to pioneer the use of anaesthesia in childbirth – and the first baby delivered under chloroform, poor unfortunate mite, was christened Anaesthesia*. It may perhaps have been due to the influence of this great man that William's thesis for his M.D. was 'On Puerperal Mania'. Certainly the training he received from Simpson must have stood him in good stead later, not only in his general practice but also in his own home, where he personally delivered all his eleven children.

The other famous name on William's certificate is that of James Syme, who revolutionised surgery, particularly where limbs were concerned, by removing, whenever possible, only the affected part instead of hacking off an entire arm or leg (without an anaesthetic, of course), as had previously been the practice. Many a patient literally owed life and limb to Syme's innovations.

To appreciate fully the tremendous strides made by men like Syme and Simpson, and the advantage which William enjoyed under their tuition, it is interesting to consider the conditions existing at the time in even

*   When, in 1866, Simpson received a baronetcy, it was suggested by some wit that his coat of arms should be 'a wee naked bairn', with the motto, 'Does you mither know you're oot?'. This suggestion has been attributed to Sir Walter Scott, who was a friend of Simpson's, but Scott dies in 1812, fifteen years before Simpson first used chloroform in childbirth.

the greatest hospitals of the day, and the difficulties under which these avant garde surgeons had to work. Syme, in his early days, was guilty of exhuming corpses for his experiments. It was, after all, only a few years since the nefarious activities of the resurrectionists had been stamped out. At least Syme's bodies were already dead; he did not hasten their end, as had Burke and Hare. Surgery still retained many of the practices of the Middle Ages. Bleeding was the general panacea, and the Lancet of 23rd March, 1844 advertised:

Case of cupping instruments	£2 13s 6d
Best bleeding lancets	£1 1s 0d

Syme, as a young man, got himself into hot water with his superiors by prescribing nourishing food and porter for a half starved patient instead of bleeding him. Unfortunately for the patient, Syme was not allowed to continue the treatment, the young man was bled – and thereupon died.

A comparison between the Annual Reports of the Edinburgh Royal Infirmary and the Radcliffe Infirmary at Oxford for 1843, when William qualified, shows how far in advance was the former of the other leading hospitals of the day. The Radcliffe, though forty years younger and not then a teaching hospital, was one of the foremost of English provincial hospitals. It had been opened in 1770* but in 1843 it employed only nine day nurses and one night nurse, whose total annual salaries amounted to £150 12s 7½d. One wonders who was fortunate enough to earn the odd halfpenny! Three washerwomen were paid 1s 10d a day 'with dinner and ale', and hay for the donkeys cost £6 11s 6d per annum. Other disbursements in the year were:

Leeches (728)	£12 2s 8d
Old Linen Rag	£ 4 0s 0d
Wine and spirits for the patients (232)	£24 2s 0d

Only 908 patients were admitted during the year (as compared with over 5000 at Edinburgh), but they consumed an astonishing quantity of

---

* It was founded by the Trustees of the Will of Dr. John Radcliffe, at one time Physician to Queen Anne, who had left a considerable part of his fortune to be used for charitable purposes.

bread. In the course of twelve months the hospital purchased:

For the House	57,288 lbs
For pudding	1,965 lbs
For surgical purposes	6,216 lbs

Of the 908 patients only four were diagnosed as cancer, while 101 were listed under the conveniently vague headings of diseased bladder, stomach, etc., and 157 'not referable'. Only sixteen operations were performed in the whole year.

By comparison, the Edinburgh Royal Infirmary of the 1840s seems almost modern – though anaesthesia and antisepsis were still the future – and William was indeed privileged to have been a student there during those momentous years when Scottish surgeons led the world.

What he did during the year after he qualified is uncertain, but he evidently remained in Edinburgh, possibly as a non-resident clerk or dresser, for the Infirmary's Register of Annual Tickets dated 1st November 1843, shows that he then purchased for £5 a ticket allowing him to 'walk the wards' for clinical instruction. After leaving Edinburgh he practised in North Sunderland until the end of 1847, but a letter from his father to Ann in 1846 suggests that he was not very happy there. He considered moving to Wooler, but eventually decided on Glanton, where he became assistant to a Dr Crae. After the latter's death William took over the practice single-handed, and lived alone at Glanton House until that happy day in 1859 when he met Elizabeth White and his whole life changed.

CHAPTER III

THE BRIDE'S HOME

'So fair a house'
Shakespeare: The Tempest

(i)

In the foothills of the Cheviots, between Alnwick and Wooler, are 2 little hills known as Glanton Hill and Pyke. Nestling on the slopes of Glanton Hill lies the village from which it takes its name. There was probably a settlement here in Roman times, for the Devil's Causeway, a branch of Watling Street, ran close to Glanton on its way from Wall, on the North Tyne, to the mouth of the Tweed. It was on the Pyke that, later in history, beacons were lit to give warning of danger in the days of the Border forays when the reivers from Scotland pillaged the land. In the nearby village of Whittingham there is still a pele tower (a fortified dwelling house), one of many built in the Border country as a protection against the marauding Scots.

Glanton House back door

Glanton is a pleasant village of stone cottages, with a magnificent view to the South where Whittingham, once famous for its fair, lies in the valley of the infant river Aln. To the east the fields roll away to Titlington Mount, a little heather-and-bracken covered hill, green in summer, purple and gold in autumn, and beyond it to the North Sea just over the horizon. Westward from Glanton Hill lie the Cheviots – the 'Muckle Cheviot,' half hidden by its slightly lower neighbour, Hedgehope, with the long low Dunmore at their feet, and a range of green hills stretching away to the Border. Their very names spell poetry and romance - Bla' Weary, Cushat Law, Black Hag, Bloody Bush Edge, and Skirl Naked high above the Happy Valley. As a child I was taken by my Aunts to visit

13

two old ladies in Wooler, and noticed on the parlour wall a lurid painting of purple mountains and swirling mists. 'Where is that?' I asked. 'Well, dear' said the elder sister in a hushed voice, 'its really Skirl Naked, but that doesn't sound quite nice, so we just call it "A view of the Cheviots"'.

Glanton House was once the Manor, and stands at the end of the village, discreetly turning its back to the road and facing south over the lovely Whittingham Vale to Thrunton Crag and the Simonside Hills. When Elizabeth went there as a bride it looked out on a sweep of gravel and a lawn surrounded by tall elms and sycamore where, on 'gurly' days, the winds from the North Sea kept up a continuous soughing and hundreds of rooks added their cacophonous accompaniment. Beyond the lawn and hidden by a laurel hedge was a large walled garden, well stocked with soft fruit and apple trees which must have been old even then. It was divided, in the fashion of the eighteenth century, into small rectangular plots edged with box and intersected by narrow gravel paths, and remained virtually unchanged for another hundred years.

The house from the croft

A doorway bearing the date 1749 leads from the walled garden to the Croft, part of which later became a tennis court. The house itself is older, probably built in about 1691. It is a charming unpretentious stone house, typically north-country in its unadorned solidity, with several blocked up windows – a reminder of the window-tax which, surprisingly, was not abolished until 1851.* For a manor house it is small, with only two not very big living rooms. In the spacious kitchen the hooks in the ceiling remind one of the days when hams were home cured. (Later they were used for drying umbrellas). A 'back-kitchen', pantry and still room complete the kitchen quarters. William used the still-room as a consulting room and dispensary, and it was known ever after as the surgery. Most of the patients had to wait in the kitchen. The odd V.I.P. would be ushered into the drawing- room, but there were few of them, for in those days no one of any standing would attend a surgery. He expected the doctor to wait on him at home, however trivial his complaint. In fact the majority of William's patients had to be visited in their own home because, even for the humbler folk, attendance at the surgery was often impossible in the absence of any public transport in this widely scattered rural practice.

William and Elizabeth slept in one of the two front bedrooms, which had an adjoining powder closet. The other was reserved for guests, and never used by the family except in an emergency. The only other sleeping accommodation on this floor was two small bedrooms (one of which later became the 'school room') and a dressing room. There was, at that time, no bathroom, one bathed in a tub in front of the kitchen fire until, at a later date, William partitioned off one end of the landing to house a bath. This was luxury indeed – except that it had no hot water. A steep cupboard staircase led to three large attics with sloping roofs, in one of them was an enormous chimney-stack round which the small children played hide-and-seek. This garret was intended for the staff but William and Elizabeth had no resident staff and the attics were used as bedrooms for their ever-growing family. Even so, one wonders how the parents and nine children squeezed into this accommodation. Any spare space in the garret was given over to storage, and, as the years went by, became crammed from floor to ceiling with trunks, chests of drawers and other paraphernalia. All the Robertsons were (and most of them still are) hoarders, and I was faced with the heterogeneous accumulation of more than a century. But that is another story.

Tradition has it that somewhere there is a secret room, but it has never been discovered.

---

*   *The window-tax was not introduced until 1697, a proof that the house was built before that date.*

In my day there was always indoor sanitation of a rather primitive kind, but there was no such mod con when William and Elizabeth were married. The only accommodation was an earth closet hidden in a shrubbery near the house. When I was a child this was still invariably used by the male members of the family, whatever the weather, the indoor water closet being reserved exclusively for the ladies. The earth closet was a small stone building containing three wooden seats, side by side, two of normal size for father and mother and a small low one for the child. Backing onto it, but accessible only from the scullery yard, was a similar contraption with two seats for the staff. Both very matey arrangements! This relic of the past remained until 1964, when it was rebuilt – as a garage.

There were also a coach-house, a saddle room, stabling for three horses and a large granary. In the yard was the wash-house with its copper. The dovecote - privilege of a manor house - was used as a hen house by Elizabeth. A two acre field provided hay for the horses.

This, then, was the domain of which the young Elizabeth became mistress in 1860. From her trousseau she chose one of her new frilly muslin caps and put it on her shapely head, for, though only just twenty-one, she was a married woman now, and for the rest of her long life would never be seen in public without this status symbol of the matron.

(ii)

What else would Elizabeth have had in her trousseau? It was usual for a Victorian bride to have twelve of everything in the way of underwear: flannel petticoats and top petticoats, chemises and drawers edged with lace and threaded with ribbon; and, as Northumbrian winters are often severe, Elizabeth would certainly have had a good supply of warm underclothes. A diary for 1860 belonging to William's brother Alexander gives edifying advice as regards clothing. In November and December, we are told 'the body should be encased in flannel,' and even in May 'it is not well to cast off flannel during the warm days that intervene now, for rheumatism and inflammatory diseases may be the consequences.' But in July 'Take off flannel which has been worn next to the skin; the perspiration induced in hot weather is apt to cause an eruption on the skin, which is moderated by wearing calico next the skin to absorb the acrid humours from the body.'*

The diary gives further advice for the preservation of health month by month, and so dire are the hazards that one wonders how anyone survives for a twelve month. In January and February one may expect 'catarrhs and inflammatory diseases,' and sudden exposure to heat is to be avoided; the March winds check perspiration and cause croup and pulmonary complaints; in April, 'if the body be not subdued by taking medicine, cutaneous eruptions and inflammatory diseases appear...and many persons are in the habit of being bled in this month.' In May one has to be very careful indeed, for it is the time for apoplexy, and the bowels should be kept freely opened. If professional advice is not available, the treatment suggested for '<u>any</u>'** indisposition' is 'at bedtime one quarter of a grain of tartar emetic, one grain of calomel, or three grains of Dr James's powder, and one and a half grains of opium, and a brisk purgative in the morning.' And in this month 'persons of delicate constitution should avoid the evening air.' Even if one manages to survive the perils of the merry month of May, the same hazards prevail in June, with the further danger of flatulent colic, while in July wine and spirits are injurious, and temperance and a frequent change of linen are advocated. But worse is to come, for in August and September cholera and 'the diarrhoeas' are prevalent, both caused by eating the skins of stone fruit, which produce spasms and 'cholic.' Suggested remedies are castor oil and paregoric, or spirits of camphor and ammonia. October brings a return of the cutaneous diseases, which are best averted by temperance, tepid baths, friction on the skin, and the avoidance of 'asciscent' articles of food. So to November and December, with their 'consumptions, coughs and rheumatisms', when we receive our final admonition: 'Avoid the night air; and never take ardent spirits in foggy weather.'

The same diary throws an interesting light on monetary values and wages in 1860. Alexander, the farmer bought two ewes for 40s each and a tup for 46s, 69 lambs for 22s each and ewe lambs for 19s 6d. A sow was very expensive - £5 9s 0d. He paid his farm worker 12s a week until 1st February, when the wage was increased to a munificent 14s

---

*   As late as 1962 Elizabeth's youngest daughter scoured Alnwick in a vain search
       for calico suitable for camisoles.
**   The italics are mine. J.R.

until Mayday. But one could get ones hair cut for 6d, gloves were 2s a pair, socks 10d and ten stone of oatmeal cost £1 6s 6d. Alexander was a meticulous keeper of accounts; he even entered in his diary a generous donation of 1s 'to Tom Greaves in Charity.' No doubt Tom touched his forelock and told his pals what a kind employer he had.

CHAPTER IV

THE YOUNG FAMILY

'She had so many children, she didn't know what to do'
Nursery Rhyme

(i)

It can have been no easy life for Elizabeth when she moved into Glanton House. Her only means of transport was her husband's pony and trap, and in the Northumbrian winter it was often impossible to drive to Alnwick, nine miles away, across the snow bound moors, so she had to make the home self-supporting, curing hams, making preserves from the fruit in the garden, baking bread and brewing beer. During haymaking and harvest the beer was carried out to the men in the field in big brown earthenware jugs.

It was not long before the young bride began the first of her many pregnancies. The first was born a year after her marriage and was christened William, but died in infancy. The next baby was my father, William again, who was born in 1863. A year later came John, and in 1866 Emily. The next year there was another son James, but he lived for only two or three hours. There followed over the next eight years four daughters in succession – Clara, Florence, Marion and Lavinia (Ina), then two more sons, Alfred in 1876 and Conrad in 1878. In between there are several miscarriages, so for seventeen years Elizabeth was seldom free from pregnancy, while coping with the ever-increasing swarm of young children needing her attention. And she had to bring them up on a shoestring. William was a busy and popular doctor but though he had a few wealthy patients in the big houses round about, the majority were farmers living at subsistence level. They paid him as and when they could, often in kind - a pound of butter or a shoulder of lamb - but there were always many outstanding debts. Frequently William knew that he would never be paid, but, being the dedicated doctor that he was, he would never refuse to treat a patient, even when he knew the family were living in such dire poverty that he could not send in a bill. In the depth of winter he would ride up into the hills to visit shepherds in isolated farms, often cut off for weeks on end by the heavy snowstorms that blocked the roads - little more than tracks then - in the Cheviot

Hills. In summer he might take the pony and trap, accompanied by some of his young family, but up to the time of his death in 1901 he did most of his visiting on horseback.

It was a mark of the love and respect in which William was held that the landlord of Glanton House, who was one of his patients, promised that as long as a Robertson lived there the rent should never be raised. This was not legally binding, and it is to the lasting credit to the landlord's descendants that, through three generations, this 'gentleman's agreement' was honoured. Until the house was sold in 1963, my last surviving aunt was paying only £40 per annum for the house and four acres of land.

(ii)

When they were nine or ten years old, the two eldest boys, William (Will) and John (Jack) were sent to Alnwick Grammar School. During the week they lived in South Street with their maiden aunts Jane and Eliza. (Aunt Ann, now a widow, also lived in Alnwick, but had her own establishment). The boys were happy enough at school, and their aunts treated them kindly according to their lights, but they were strict and puritanical. Although William and Elizabeth were Victorian in their emphasis and discipline and religious observance, they were understanding of children and, for those days, broad minded. Not so the aunts; Sunday for them was a day of gloom. Though they did not go to the length of turning the pictures to the walls and draping them with black crepe, as had once been the custom in the most rigid north country families, they would allow no amusement in their houses on the Lord's Day. Church-going was, of course, de rigueur, and this was no hardship to Will and Jack; it was a recognised part of their life at home. But not the whole of Sunday was spent in church, and what were they to do during the rest of the day? Games, of course, were out of the question, and, if they wanted to read, then they must read the Bible, a book of sermons or some other 'good book' approved by the aunts. They must not even whistle on a Sunday. This was more than the lads could bear, and rather than endure their aunts' rigid discipline they walked home to Glanton nearly every weekend, winter and summer. In the summer no doubt they enjoyed the tramp over Alnwick Moor, famous for its strawberry beds, with its superb view of the Northumbrian countryside and a glimpse of the sea in the distance. But in Winter it was no light undertaking. It was

9 miles to Glanton, and often the moor would be deep in snow. Yet only the severest of weather would keep them in Alnwick, and it says much for the happy home life in Glanton House that the boys would make this journey twice in a weekend rather than spend it with their aunts.

The Robertson Family

Many years later when Jack was in Canada, he recalled in a letter to Emily the dreary weekends when he and Will were obliged to stay in Alnwick:

> *'What a heinous sin this letter-writing would have been on one of the catechism-and-cold-meat-dinner Sabbaths at Alnwick, when we read good books and gained nothing by it but bad tempers. On those days it was a grievous sin to smile – cheerfulness was banished for a time, in fact was never fully restored till about the middle of the week, and even then a Wednesday evening prayer meeting sometimes came in the way to frighten us once more. Of course you will say I ought not to write like this, ought to remember it was for my good (?) etc., etc., but I cannot help remembering the delightful relief it was to get home on Sunday and loll about the garden or lie on my back in the field or sometimes take a stroll in the lanes in your company, Miss, on which occasions I dare say I was more of an angel than when racking my brains over Dr. Watts or Doddridge in the stuffy sanctimonious silence of South Street.'*

During the week, however, the boys were allowed some amusement, and one welcome diversion was the Hiring Fair. In 1878 Jack wrote to tell his parents about it.

> *'We were at the "Tomahawk" Minstrels on Wednesday evening and enjoyed it very much. The town is pretty full today. There are a good few people in to get hired, and a few shows, shooting galleries etc., etc.'*

Another exciting annual event in Alnwick was the football match held on Shrove Tuesday, which was a general holiday. The game followed no recognised rules, it was a free-for-all in which any of the townsfolk could take part, the more the merrier, and Will and Jack joined in the fun. The ball was kicked from the Castle gate right through the town – down Narrowgate and Bondgate Within, through Hotspur Tower, along Bondgate Without, ending up in the river.

(iii)

Meanwhile Emily and Clara were having lessons from their mother. Girls were not often sent away to school in those days, and in any case William could not afford it. Such money as could be spared must be spent on educating the boys. But William's sister Ann was a well-to-do widow, and it was through her generosity that the two eldest girls eventually received a good education. At first, they went to school in Alnwick, where they, too, lived with their aunts, then to Abney Park College for Ladies at Stamford Hill, in London. In 1879, while they were still at Alnwick, Emily celebrated her thirteenth birthday, and Elizabeth wrote;

> *'May God bless you, my dear child, and grant that each year may find you not only older, but wiser and better, and travelling that narrow road that leads to our heavenly home...I hope you are settling nicely and liking your lessons.'*

When the girls left Alnwick, William took them to London and met their Headmistress, Miss Richards. A letter from their mother written soon after reads;
> *'Papa seems to like Miss Richards, and I hope you will be happy*

while under her care and be good and obedient girls, remembering how much lies with yourselves and your conduct as to how you get on. At first the discipline may be trying to you, but you must pray for strength to bear it willingly and patiently, for your own good…It has always been my heart's wish for you, that you should get a little more education than it was in our power to give and we can never be sufficiently grateful to Aunt Ann for her great kindness and the sacrifice she is making for you. God has been very good to us.'

Emily and Clara must have felt very lonely when they said good-bye to their father and were left alone in the big city so far from home. Fortunately there lived near the school a Mrs Barber, an old friend of the family, who kept a kindly eye and frequently invited them to her house.

Eighteen months later, in December 1880, Elizabeth wrote to the girls saying that they would have to be content with 'a very short scrap' that week. There had been a domestic crisis. It was 'washing week' and everything was drying in the kitchen when at 2 o'clock the sweep arrived to do the kitchen chimney. Papa had said he would be in to dinner at 2.30, and there was all the washing to move to the back kitchen, where a fire had to be lit. There had been heavy snow, and the back door was blocked up and had to be cleared. 'We were in a lopper' was Elizabeth's mild comment. Yet the 'very short scrap' ran into ten pages, and Elizabeth chided herself for not having the girls ties ready to send. 'I will do so tomorrow,' she promised. ' Did Emily take her scarlet crepe? I will send a mauve one for Clara.' On top of everything she had five young children to cope with, Florence, the eldest, being eight years old and Conrad, the baby of the family, only two.

Washing day always caused a major upheaval, even without the sweep and the snow. A woman from the village came every two or three weeks to help with it, and what a wash it must have been! It is clear from Elizabeth's letters that the two girls at school, and Will and Jack (also in London by this time) all sent their washing home, so there were eleven people's clothes to launder, not to mention the damask table cloths and napkins, linen sheets and towels. A fire was lit under the copper in the wash-house, and when the washing was done it had to be mangled. The mangle was kept in the coach house; no other room was big enough.

It consisted of an enormous wooden tray, about six feet long and four feet wide, set on large rollers. The tray was filled with huge stones, and a wide leather strap attached it to an overhead cross-piece. By means of a handle at the side this cumbersome contraption was moved backwards and forwards across the rollers – an operation that called for considerable physical effort from two people. After being mangled the washing was spread out to dry on the hedge beside the tennis court. If it rained, the clothes had to be draped all over the kitchen, the back kitchen and the outbuildings. Ironing took several hours, and three or four flat irons were kept hot on the kitchen range. The mangle had ceased to be used in my day, and the size of the wash gradually decreased as the family left home, but otherwise the process varied little over a hundred years.

At the end of 1884 Emily and Clara sat for examinations. They both passed very creditably, and received a gratified letter from their mother. They evidently thought that, having this scholastic achievement behind them, they could afford to indulge more in the handicrafts at which they were to prove so gifted in later life, but Elizabeth disagreed;

> *'About trying for the prize for needlework, I really think you had better not think of it. You have a great many lessons and what spare time you may have I would rather you occupied in doing the Cushion for your Aunt or any other little thing for her. You can try to excel in needlework after your return home. At present you have as much to do as is good for you.'*

But before she closed the letter she relented a little:

> *'If you really would like some calico, I will... send it, but we think you have as much to do as you can do properly.'*

Elizabeth herself was never short of sewing. In one letter to the girls she said that she had thirty pairs of stockings to mend, and found it slow work. 'It is always 4 o'clock before I can get sat down and then lessons come on after tea (for the younger children).'

In another letter Elizabeth told the girls about a village concert:

> *'Papa, Marion, and I went up to Mr. Wood's concert on Friday*

evening and were very much disappointed. It was a miserable affair. His class did not do badly, but he allowed several of the people about to sing, and spoiled the whole business.'

Young Marion, writing to her sisters at the same time, was more outspoken:

'Oh! I have never heard such singing before it was perfectly horrible most of it was it was worst when the men sang. Mrs Magie Mary and Ellen McGhie went with us both Mrs and Magie was perfectly shocked.'

Though her spelling and punctuation might be shaky, she already had very decided views on singing! She later had quite a good voice herself, and was in the church choir until she was in her seventies. Having got the concert off her chest, she carried on with the news:

'Poor Ellen has such a sore foot with a broken chilblane. Aunt Dixon sent a little box of stuff for to make the hens lay I hope it will make them lay she says there hens didnt lay till they got some of the stuff. I do not think I have any more to say.'

But she added an indignant postscript:

'They are shuting Pigeons today the men aught to be shot themselves for it,'

- a view held by all my aunts until their dying day.

In 1884 Emily, now 18, began a new exercise book for Composition, and for some reason inscribed her name on the flyleaf as 'Emily Robertson Esq.' Her essays, for all their immaturity and purple patches, already show the ready pen, the love of nature and whimsical humour that were to blossom in later years.

'Inexpressibly beautiful in Winter, with its pure white covering of snow, looking as if the angels, in order that all might be in harmony with the blessed time of year, had lent their own pure robes for a season to cover the barrenness of earth.'

And in an essay entitled 'It was an evening in Eden,'

> 'Loveliest hour even in that sweet clime where all was lovely. The sun was sinking into the west in all his golden glory, but he sank slowly, as if sad at parting with so beautiful a scene even until morning, and ever and anon as he sank behind the hills, he seemed to be endowed with fresh power and brilliancy and to return as if for another glimpse of the fair garden and bathe the flowery vales and dark cypress groves in floods of light. Perhaps it was a presentiment of coming evil which made him linger so long that evening.'

Emily left school later that year, but Clara stayed on for another four years until she, too, was nearly eighteen. In June 1887, the year of Queen Victoria's golden jubilee, William wrote to her;

> 'I shall be glad to hear how you spent the Jubilee day...What a splendid display there has been in London, as we see by the papers. Here we had a very nice day of it on the hill and everything went off well till the very end, after the bonfire was almost done too, near midnight, when the news came to the village that three or four miscreants set fire to the fox cover of whin...so vexing to us all who had enjoyed the day so pleasantly, and how angry Mr Pawson (the land owner) is you may imagine. I wish the villains may yet be found out and brought to justice...We had a splendid bonfire and a few nice fire works on a small scale, and we saw about a score of fires on the surrounding eminences...We had a tolerably good band from Alnwick who played some capital dance music and plenty of dancing there was on the grass between the two hills. The tea and refreshments were good and ample and pleased everyone. It is calculated there were nearly a thousand people young and old on the Hill.'

William told Clara that her aunt Jane, who had had a stroke in May, was very ill and not expected to live long. Elizabeth, taking little Ina with her, had gone to Alnwick by post gig and stayed the night. Ina, aged only eleven, was left behind to help her aunt Eliza. A month later Jane was still alive, and better physically, but Elizabeth said that her mind was badly shattered. 'She gets very much excited and bad to manage...Aunt

Eliza is very poorly indeed. She looks so thin and worn out, and you know Aunt Ann does not take much trouble or try to relieve her as she might.' Poor Eliza! Ever since the time long ago when she had been sent to housekeep for her uncle in Stirling, she had always been the dogsbody. During the many years that she and Jane had lived together in Alnwick, it was always Eliza, the younger sister, who was expected to shoulder most of the burdens of housekeeping, who organised their move from South Street to Prudhoe Street, who waited upon Jane, while Ann, well-to-do and comfortably installed in her own house, gave little help. It was probably fortunate for all concerned that Jane did not live long.

After leaving school, Clara stayed at home for a while, sometimes going to Alnwick for a few days to visit her aunts. On these occasions various members of the family frequently gave her commissions. During one such visit she received an urgent request from Emily:

> 'When you come home will you bring me a sailor hat from Archbold or anywhere you can get it...I think you will get a very decent one for 1/ or 1/3 or less. I want a white one with pale blue ribbon.

> P.S. If possible, as much as lies in you, send the hat tomorrow. You might go to the station at the two and the 7 trains, and anyone man or woman-body would quite willingly bring it if they were coming to Glanton...You see I'd like to put on my shirt on Friday and can't with my other hats.'

How typical of the impatient and slightly dictatorial Emily!

Clara was not going home until Saturday, and though by this time there was a railway her father evidently took it for granted that she would walk the nine miles from Alnwick - but he did offer to meet her at Bolton with the 'conveyance' to save her the last three miles.

Chapter V

LONDON INTERLUDE

'Long in populous city pent'
Milton: Paradise lost

(i)

While the two eldest girls were still at school, Will and Jack had also gone to London. Will was determined to follow in his father's footsteps and study medicine, but no money was available, and in those days there were, of course, no grants for students. Will therefore took a job in a City office to earn the money for his medical training. He worked first with Messrs. Burdett and Co in the Commercial Road. He was little more than an office boy, sticking on stamps and running errands – he was only about sixteen – and earned a few shillings a week. Jack was an apprentice at the warehouse of Messrs. Copestake, Hughes, Crampton and Co. in Bow Church Yard, and earned nothing at all.

William had been to London, but did not know it very well, so he borrowed a map from the Glanton minister to see exactly where his sons were living and working. From this he discovered that Will was three miles from Jack's lodgings in Charterhouse Square and three and a half miles from the warehouse. He hoped, nevertheless, that they could arrange to meet on Saturday afternoons, and took pains to find out, perhaps from the minister, the easiest way for Will to travel to the City:

> *'He will take the tramway from about Aldgate Pump .... He will get a ride for 1d or 2d ...... Again, Stepney Station is, I understand, very near you, which would take you to Fenchurch Street quite near the Bank. These are all new conveniences since I visited the Commercial Road. There were only omnibuses in those days.'*

William apparently regarded the tram as a modern improvement!

Soon after he went to London, Will had a letter from a Miss Scott of Sunderland, one of the families of Scott brothers, the pottery manufacturers. She was an old friend of Elizabeth's and all the children called her 'Auntie Scott', though she was, in fact, no relation. She had lived in London for some years, and hoped that Will and Jack would see all the sights of the metropolis. 'You will find even the East End very nice when you get out of Whitechapel,' she wrote. 'The Bow Road is a fine, open street and the Victoria Park worth seeing.' She enclosed a half sovereign for each of the boys.

Will did not stay long with Burdett and Co. He obtained a post in the offices of Copestake, Hughes, Crampton and Co., in whose warehouse Jack was working, and the brothers were able to share lodgings in Charterhouse Square. Although this was a much happier arrangement, and Will eventually rose to quite a senior position, he did not like office work and only his determination to study medicine made him stick to it. In a letter to Emily he complained:

> 'Everything is as dismal as possible here and the prospect of months of hard work before any holiday is dismal indeed. Not that I object to hard work but ours is so disagreeable and we are so far away from you all.'

To this he added a hurried postscript:

> 'You will find a bag of worms on the ledge above the window in the hen house. Please put them out if they are not dead. Don't forget to put the large minnow into a new bottle and fresh spirits.'

The 'City gent' was still a child at heart.

When he finished his day's work at the office, Will spent most of his spare time preparing himself for his medical career, either studying in his lodgings or attending the 'Institution'. 'Poor Will,' wrote Jack to Emily in 1883, 'he seems to be studying hard, though what is to be the upshot of all this head-scratching, brow-puckering and general studious demeanour, I can't say. I do hope he will make something out and that the good name of William Robertson, Esq., M.D., is not to become extinct yet a wee.'

Both boys hated urban life, and Jack wrote to Emily, 'You seem to be kept busy just now with hay making, ginger beer manufacturing, etc.,

etc.......I would not object to that at all. It is better and altogether more suitable employment than this confounded quill-driving.' On their day off they liked to go out into the country whenever possible. A letter from Jack to Emily describes one such outing on a Good Friday to Epping Forest, a favourite haunt, where they walked from 10 am to 6.30 pm. 'I have no doubt there were lots of folk in the forest,' he said, 'though you only came across a few now and then'. They somehow lost each other while Will, who was always a keen entomologist, was chasing butterflies, and Jack decided that he would have to go back to London by himself. But he had no money – it was all in Will's pocket – and London was twelve miles away. Though he had already tramped for eight and a half hours in the forest, he had just made up his mind to walk home when Will – and the money – turned up.

Jack's first letter

While the boys were in London, William was thinking of leaving Glanton. He could not make enough money there to support his large family, he found the place 'dull and wretched' and he was suffering from the vagaries of the Northumbrian climate. In a letter to Will Aunt Ann, too, expressed the hope that her brother would hear of something in the south, 'a better Practice – his ability is lost at Glanton and so many changes in the place within the last few years.' William had London in mind, but Jack, writing to Emily, said:

> 'I hope Papa won't come to London just because we are here. I don't think he would care for it much, though he talks of it being such a fine place.'

Jack was probably right, and certainly all the young people would have been heart-broken at leaving Glanton, where they had spent such a happy childhood. At the beginning of 1884 Jack recalled nostalgically the day when he and Will and Emily, always a close-knit trio, had led a free, uninhibited life at Glanton House:

> 'My dearest Sister and partner in many a mischievous enterprise in days gone by,' he wrote to Emily, 'I wish you a very happy New Year – a happier one, if can be, than even those of Auld Lang Syne when "we three" went about as a very trinity of mischief …..Things have changed wi' us since the time when we used to inhabit the hut in the stackyard and cook apples and potatoes there, imagining ourselves veritable Robinson Crusoes (and I dare say we <u>did</u> resemble him in our semi-savage tastes), since we took a fiendish delight in choking up M-'s* wash-house chimney and listening to the ejaculations of surprise and disgust from below.'

Nothing came of William's proposed move, and though during the coming years he often talked of leaving Glanton he continued to live and practice there until the end of his life.

(ii)

In January 1883, Elizabeth was ill, and it was William who wrote the weekly letter to the two young men in London. He sent them some novels, but did not think much of them himself. 'I do not think I would encounter one of Lytton's novels again. They are wearisome and long-winded.' Nor, it seems did he quite approve of the boys' enthusiasm for music, which led them frequently to attend the new Gilbert and Sullivan operas, and concerts where they heard great singers like Adelina Patti:

---

*   *The Marchioness,' the children's nickname for their neighbour at the Villa.*

'You certainly have a fair share of music of one kind and another. I wish you may not get too much of a good thing and neglect more important and improving exercises. Now is the time to avail yourselves of every advantage that you can see or hear of. You will never have so good a chance again, perhaps, and, my dear Boys, do look out and try to get hold of improving and elevating literature at least and avoid all trashy stuff... Aim at what is really noble and manly, and learn how little you know as yet .... No mark of <u>true greatness</u> like genuine humility, but <u>only wise men know this.</u>'

William was a true son of the Reverend James of Wooler, but a very loving and understanding parent. In later years Will was to write to Emily, 'Rarely, I think, have any children had so dear and good a father.'

William went on to tell them that the local innkeeper was likely to lose his licence for drunk and disorderly conduct and assaulting a policeman. 'Our village is becoming more and more disreputable,' he said. Perhaps this was one reason why he wanted to leave it. He gave them news of Ben, his beloved pony. Ben was kept mainly for William to ride when visiting his patients, but he was ridden and adored by all the children.

'I intend to <u>ride</u> the pony a good deal more' he told them. *'He is tremendously plucky now that he is clipped, and indeed I have had to reduce his corn, but on his back I can manage him to a T. Of course I must drive a good deal but I am not so afraid now of his tumbling down. He is a rare plucky fellow and if only I mind him over the hills I think he will carry me a while yet.'*

Ben served William for nearly two more years, but at the end of 1884 he wrote to the girls:

'Old Ben is very up on his wind now. He is getting worse and worse. I have a horse in prospect but whether it will suit remains yet to be seen. If I do not fall in [with it] very soon I do not know what I shall do, for poor Ben is indeed hard up.'

It was a sad day for them all when old Ben departed, but his successor, Polly, soon wheedled her way into their hearts.

In March 1883, Elizabeth paid a visit to London and to her cousin in the Isle of Wight, leaving the seventeen-year-old Emily, home for the holidays, to run the house and look after the children, the youngest of whom, Conrad, was only five. Emily took it all in her stride, and in her letters to Elizabeth one can detect a certain pride in her ability to act as temporary 'mother'. 'The children are behaving splendidly and not a bit of bother' she wrote. She even spent one night alone in the house with the children, when William was obliged to stay overnight with a sick patient at Beanley, several miles away. Emily was quite unperturbed, but the village folk thought her very brave and 'uncanny'.

She arranged for the dining room and kitchen chimneys to be swept while her mother was away, but the roads were blocked by snow and the sweep could not get through. She hoped he would come next day, as they had to live in the drawing room and back kitchen. In the dining-room 'the pictures are down and the carpets are up and the ornaments stuffed away and the chairs heaped up and shrouded in drapery of various kinds and colours and the grate deprived of its ashes yawns dismally and the clock ticks solemnly from behind its white pall…. The drawing-room is a capital place for the children, where without "by your leave" they calmly appropriate everything from the lustres and other mantel-piece ornaments to the poker and tongs as their own property.' The lustres were vases of rose-red glass with white pendants like icicles that tinkled when you swung them – lovely playthings, no doubt, but one shudders nowadays to think of these treasured pieces of Victoriana being used as toys by a swarm of rumbustious children. They did, however, live to tinkle another day.

In another letter Emily told her mother that 'we got some patterns of stuff for Alfy's blouse ……I'm going to bind his old one round the bottom tonight and I've got the sleeves patched.' Emily was having a busy time. She added a postscript: 'The bairns are behaving their very best.' This was as well, for, in addition to coping with the family, Emily had to entertain a houseguest. He was a Mr Gibbon, a poet, generally referred to by Emily as 'Mr G' or 'King Ceteweyo', the latter nickname probably due to his vast dimensions, for, like Ben Jonson, he weighed twenty stone. The Zulu king was much in the news at the time, having been brought to England as a prisoner in the previous year, and, at the time when Emily was writing, there was an outcry in the country which

33

led to his restoration to his African kingdom. 'Mr G' was not <u>persona grata</u> with Emily:

> *'What'll I do wi' him if Papa's out, for it's clear he can't accompany him. There's no room and the gig would go smash and as for the pony it would never be seen more. Fancy a <u>Poet</u> 20 stone weight: I'll have to do the agreeable as well as I can, but can or does he talk anything except about poetry and sentiment?'*

'Mr. G.' was not likely to lose any weight while at Glanton House. The day before he arrived Emily baked a scone for tea, as there was 'not a bit of bread in the house,' but she put off making the bread in order to have it really new for 'Mr.G.' She gave her mother her proposed menus for his dinners:

> *'Tuesday – roast beef and apple tart, peas, beer, etc.*
> *Wednesday – pie, light pudding, vegetables*
> *Thursday – something, vegetables, jam dumpling.'*

For tea she would make 'singin' hinnies' (Northumbrian girdle cakes).

One day the minister called, and 'Mr. G.' grew quite loving, and finally embraced him, almost hiding him from view in so doing, to the great delight and amusement of the children and discomfort of the said minister.

When at last the good poet departed, Emily heaved a sigh of relief.

> *'His most Serene Highness King Cetewayo has departed, every stone of him. I'm glad he's away. He's a regular bore and he smokes like a kiln, feeds like a sponge, talks like a pen-gun, snores like a grampus, melts like a half-done piece of beef and kisses the Blarney stone awfully. He talks everlastingly about Poets, but doesn't like Byron or Tom Moore or Mr. Gladstone.'*

A graphic but not very flattering pen-portrait:

'Mr. G.' died in 1888. 'He will be missed from the race of Giants,' wrote Jack. 'He would need an enormous coffin!'

(iii)

In October 1883, the day after his nineteenth birthday, Jack completed his apprenticeship and wrote to Emily rejoicing in his comparative freedom. She had sent him a copy of Robert Burns' poems as a birthday present, and he showed his appreciation by writing to her in Lallanes:

> 'Weel, the morn's mornin' I suppose I'll hae bid fareweel o' the chains o' apprenticeship, and may gang aboot in a' the glory o' my sax fit – feelin' mair like a free mon than I did afore. Fancy sarvin' my mony maisters for three haill years for no sae muckle as a bawbee o' wage. It seems as gin I'd gane and thrawn away the time for the fun o' the thing …. But now I may consider mysell "passin' rich on twenty pun' (or sae) a year." Twenty pun' nae less! Whatever will I dae wi' it a'? It'll wear oot my pooches, chok up my muckle black box and maybe Bill's kist as weel. Twenty pun'! I'll hae to tell C.H.C. that it's ower guid o' them, that I cana take it a', that they'd far better keep it themsels wha hae sae little – !!!'

Even Will was not earning a great deal, so it was seldom that they could make the expensive journey to Glanton except for their fortnight's holiday in the summer. In any case it was too far to travel for the weekend; they had to work every Saturday morning, and even Bank Holidays, apart from Easter, were limited to one day. In 1883 they spent Easter at Ryde, in the Isle of Wight, where Elizabeth's cousin, 'Uncle Dixon', lived, but, though they enjoyed the holiday and appreciated the island's scenery, they still longed for their Northumbrian hills. Sometimes they were invited to join their sisters at Mrs. Barber's house for a soiree musicale. 'You must tell them to put on their best clothes and white fronts, etc.', Elizabeth wrote to Emily, and the girls were to be sure to get 'a pair of nice silk gloves.'

Jack was even more frustrated by the restrictions of office life than Will. The latter was sustained by the prospect of eventually attaining his ambition of becoming a doctor, but Jack had no such incentive. He had no particular career in view, and his only desire was to be free from the shackles of City life. He was always to be a rolling stone, and in 1884 was already dreaming of the time when he could say good-bye to London and start afresh overseas.

35

'If I had a few pounds,' he wrote to Emily, *'I'd be off to one of the colonies like a shot, and a year or two will most likely see me a long day's march from London. Will, poor chap, seems to me to be over head and ears in work, half smothered in living and dead languages, mathematics and all the rest. I hope this close application to study will have its reward – it certainly deserves it.'*

Meanwhile he and Will made the best of their unwilling sojourn in the City, and saw all the sights of the metropolis, some of which their Presbyterian parents might not have approved:

'Tell it not in Gath,' Jack confided to his sister, *'nor to our good minister – we went to a Roman Catholic church last night (the Italian church, Hatton Garden). It was a "grand special evening service" in the advertisement and the admission was 6d each. The service was fine enough with its processions and incense and all the rest of it, but the main attraction was the performance of the Stabat Mater (Rossini) after the service …. Altogether we were in church from 7 till half past nine. How all this grand music and the incense etc. would shake the nerves of Mr. Davidson [the Glanton minister]. I believe he would either protest against it there and then in good honest style or would faint from excess of horror and disgust.'*

The lads were very fond of the theatre and, whenever they could afford it, queued for seats in the gallery to see such great actors and actresses as Sir Henry Irving, Ellen Terry and Sarah Bernhardt. Fifty years later Jack could still recall the excitement of those nights:

'I was greatly interested in the articles on dear Ellen Terry in John o' London. Well do I remember seeing her charming acting and hearing her glorious <u>voice</u> in the palmy days of Irving at the Lyceum – as Juliet, Beatrice, Olivia and Margaret (Faust). Will, no doubt, has not forgotten those nights in the gods, hot and smelling of humanity and orange peel, but nights of real enjoyment and romance. The play was the thing – nothing else mattered. There was an old woman who sold pigs' feet for the delectation of the fashionable patrons of the Gallery. Ah me!

36

How times have changed since the '80s, and not altogether for the better.'

By the end of 1884 Jack had begun to make definite plans for his first venture abroad. When his parents heard that he proposed to go to Canada they were greatly distressed, and Elizabeth wrote to the two girls in London:

> *Jack seems bent upon going to Canada, and much as we regret his choice, and dread the parting, would not like to stand in his way, but really I do not see any kindness in Alec Young's offer [Alec Young was a farmer], he offers <u>board and lodging</u> for a year – in return for which he expects a full man's work, <u>no wage</u> mind – this is of course, with board and lodging, a full wage could not be expected, but if he receives <u>nothing</u> – at the end of the year he is thrown a <u>pauper</u> nothing in his pocket, upon his own resources – nothing even to keep himself in clothes or pocket money – depend upon it Alec knows what he is about when he makes the offer, and Jack would have to work hard – but where the money is to come from to send him away I know not, unless Uncle Dixon advances it as he offered to do when I was there – but I see little prospect of Jack being able to repay the loan if he is to work for <u>nothing</u> – Oh dear! It is a heart-breaking thought, and yet I do not think dear Jack will settle to anything else. Had we only been able to send him out with a nice sum in his pocket I would not have opposed it – I do not dread the voyage so much as your Papa does – but I see nothing at the end of it.'*

Jack's proposal was obviously a bombshell. He was very young, and in those days the long voyage and the venture into the unknown were not to be lightly undertaken, even if one had money. That Elizabeth, normally so calm, so trusting in Providence, should write this frantic letter to her two young school-girl daughters is evidence of her distress. The lack of punctuation, the frequent underlining (a Victorian habit, but one in which she seldom indulged) are quite unlike her usual style, and reflect the fear and heartache that Jack's imminent departure was causing.

In the event he did not go to Canada for another three years. Perhaps his parents dissuaded him. He was still in London at the beginning of 1886 when one Sunday he wrote to Emily:

> *'No doubt you have been to the "Meetin' " this morning …. and heard a good solid sermon, not the wishy-washy slops which are doled out in too many of the churches, but regular slices of doctrine and exhortation which so well suit the vigorous appetites of the sturdy and serious Northumbrians. Cannot you fancy the disgust of some of those plaided shepherds who walk their seven miles each way to Kirk if they were to hear a ten minutes sing-song from some of these delicate and exquisite curates with no hair on their faces or brains in their heads???'*

He had met his schoolgirl sister, just back from her Christmas holiday at Glanton.

> *'You know we saw Tim [Clara] last Saturday…She is as quiet as ever, and I think perfectly harmless. She looks well after her holiday, tho' she told me she almost never went out of doors – and was just as happy, I daresay, such is her nature. But I should like to have heard of your going home for a month and sticking indoors, whatever the weather, having never once got wet feet, or had a cataract of melting snow down your back – if it was winter – having never once torn your dress in the Denes or lost your hat on the hill, if it was summer, having never got into a scrape of any sort for the very good reason that you never tried. Well, what is one man's (or woman's) meat is another man's (or woman's) poison. When we get home in the summer are you on for a tramp in the grey morning thro' fields to Branton, on to Ingram and Linhope once more, as on that memorable occasion two years or more ago when we buoyed ourselves up with hope of the sun's appearance thro' the wet mist hour after hour, and he never appeared, when we sang cheering dirges on the stones near Alnham Moor to revive our drooping spirits and dripping, or at least, damp, bodies, when we at last resolved to make the best of it, and as proof of this resolve sat down cheerfully to our broiled trout at the Linn, and when I daresay you at least came in for a scolding on our arrival home again.'*

Here Jack puts in a nutshell the difference in temperament between his two eldest sisters – the lively, tomboy Emily and the quiet, peace-loving Clara – a difference which was to be apparent all through their lives, but which did not prevent them from remaining devoted companions.

Jack's dream of tramping over the hills to Linhope with Emily was not fulfilled, for long before summer came he was several thousand miles away.

(iv)

There was always a close bond between Will and his eldest sister, and he wrote to her frequently. They both read widely and exchanged views on their latest reading, and they shared a keen sense of humour, a lively wit and an intense love of Glanton and all that their home stood for. In 1884 Will consulted Emily about a birthday present for their mother. 'Perhaps,' he suggested, 'an album for Cabinet Photos would be nice. I don't think Mamma has one. I have seen some very pretty ones about, all illuminated round about where the photos go.' Typically Victorian, in fact!

Will often subjected Emily to gently teasing:

> 'To my most dearly beloved Sister, Her Most Gracious Majesty the queen of the Guinea Pigs, Rabbits and sundry other representatives and types and various families, genera and species too numerous to mention, I send greeting.' (Emily was always passionately fond of animals and, in her young day, kept a miniature menagerie of small pets.) 'It is with the greatest sense of obligation to you that I acknowledge myself to be the recipient of your letter dated April. I can assure you that I feel and appreciate to the utmost the great honour you confer upon me by your gracious forbearance and magnanimous condescension in deigning to expend so much of your time and talent in writing to your – I won't say what kind of a – brother.'

And again:

> 'Your epistle to hand last week filled as usual with the surplus exuberance of your fertile imagination to the brim. It was also

as usual written on so many green and grey and blue and white ½ sheets of paper that I hardly knew in what order to take them, while the ink was laid on as thickly that I suppose you would have to lay them out on the hedge to dry and anyone happening to look "over the garden wall" from the Villa garden would think that a lot of young Joseph's coats of many colours had just been born..... I wish you would take the precaution to number your sheets so that one might read your voluminous documents with greater facility.'

This was written when Emily was sixteen, but with regard to letter writing she never changed. She wrote wonderful entertaining and witty letters, but to the end of her days they were scrawled on any odd bits of paper she could lay hands on. I once gave her a large box of stamped notepaper for Christmas. I suppose she did use it, but never to me. Always I received scraps of varying hues and sizes, and never did she number the pages. Impatient by nature, with an intellect like quicksilver, she must rattle off her letters as the thoughts came to her on whatever material was at hand. The same trait was apparent when she was engaged in kitchen chores. If she was making tea she could not wait for the kettle to boil, her jam was never properly set, and many a glass dish she broke from pouring boiling liquid into it.

Some of Will's letters to Emily were written on long strips of bright pink paper only about four inches wide but at least two feet in length. One suspects that they were purloined from the office. It seemed to be a case of two kettles calling each other black, for, in spite of her own predilection for odd scraps of paper of strange colours, Emily protested against Will's choice of stationery. 'Since you have such an insuperable objection to the paper I have written to you on lately,' he replied, 'I have commenced on some green paper which I hope will suit you to a T. I hope you like green tea, and I remember you were always fond of cabbages, about which you used to sing and compose sonnets.' What a pity these sonnets have not survived! There followed five closely written pages describing Will's visit to Maskelyne and Cook's, with graphic descriptions of the uncanny and sometimes hair-raising turns put on by those famous conjurers. What wonderful letter-writers the Victorians were! How often, nowadays, would a brother trouble to write eight packed pages to his young sister? Not that Emily could expect this every time. ' It won't be often that I will write so much at one time to you. Don't let me hear you complain any more, do you hear? I won't submit to it…I hope the next letter will show an improvement in you.'

In 1887 Emily was twenty-one, and Will wrote her an affectionate letter of congratulation:

> *'I wish to congratulate you on having reached the age of discretion and that you are no longer… an infant, and I hope you will accept the little book I send and that though deep it will please your no longer infantile mind….Wishing you long life and many happy birthdays (Hundreds of 'em).'*

Emily did live to be nearly ninety-two.

It was later in this year that the railway from Alnwick to Coldstream was completed. When, four years earlier, William had told the boys that Glanton was to have a station, Will, far away in London, had shown little interest. 'I don't suppose I shall trouble the railway much or take a daily trip to see how it is getting on,' he wrote. 'We must do like the red man and retire West before the march of civilization.'. But when the railway opened on 1st September 1887, Will and Jack, home for their fortnight's holiday, took the first two tickets to be issued from Glanton station. They travelled as far as Hedgeley, the next station, whence they walked back to Glanton. The following month William and Elizabeth made their first trip to Alnwick by rail. 'It certainly is an improvement upon the old system of driving across the Moor,' Elizabeth wrote to Clara, 'especially in the Winter months. Papa was a little nervous on the return journey. We certainly did come down to Edlingham at a reeling pace!'

CHAPTER VI
LIFE WITH THE MOUNTIES

'To the wilderness I wander'
Anon: Tom o'Bedlam

Jack in Canadian Mounted Rifles uniform

In 1888 Jack at last went to Canada, and in April of that year he gave Emily a glimpse of his life there:

'The bill of fare is as follows, with slight variations.
Breakfast – bread and butter, pork or eggs, tea.
Dinner – pork, potatoes, pie or stewed prunes or apples, bread and butter, tea.
Supper – bread and butter, eggs or pork, stewed fruit or pies, tea.
The national food, you will see, is pork in various forms, and the national beverage tea, which is served at all meals. How I would enjoy a cup of coffee and a bit of brown bread! …. I see the boundless prairie, studded with scrub and small "slews" or ponds, wild ducks and geese, ground squirrels and gophers (little striped animals like squirrels), shanties of wood, and stables of straw, the sun by day – how different from England! – And the stars by night, these last assisted in their illuminating business by numerous fires all round on the prairie.'

This was written while Jack was with Alec Young, and is the only record extant of that first difficult year. In 1890 he joined the North West Mounted Police, and by 1892 had become an old hand at the pioneering life. He wrote to Emily:

'I believe, if the truth were known, I am a far more "domesticated" creature than you are now, and I am sure will make a model husband. I will be able to do the baking while the wife talks scandal with her next-door neighbour, and trifle with the washing at a pinch, if necessary. Do you think you could recommend me to some girl in the neighbourhood who is looking for just such a useful sort of man? You might mention that I am a fair all-round cook and can dish up the festive bean and the succulent sowbelly to perfection.'

The following year, when Emily had gone to Germany, Jack wrote a long letter to his sister – both of them now exiles in a foreign land:

'A couple of dancing bears passed through our "town" and the keepers were German, I think, from the way they butchered their English. They made the poor brutes "climb de polegram" (telegraph pole) …..Perhaps you do not know that I am a bit of a musician. My instrument of torture is the tuneful banjo … What sort of climate have you in Silesia? I rather think it is severe, but only from an English standpoint, certainly not from a Canadian … This section of country – S. Alberta – is supposed to be a balmy region and on this 20th day of April the ground is covered with snow and the frost at night would be considered severe in England. There is no growth on the prairie and the general appearance of the country is that of a howling desolation … The old house must seem "kinder" lonely these days, and I would like to have a look in and take the old folks by surprise.'

Food still played an important part in an otherwise monotonous existence:

'I am cook this week, and have been busy all morning making pies of the "kill me quick" pattern – four containing dried peaches and two custard. Yesterday I constructed a bulletproof "duff" which the

ostrich-stomached lads demolished. They still live ... Our staples at present are sowbelly and beans and dried apples. Potatoes are not obtainable, and for fresh meat we are entirely dependent on the gun. We have had a few geese and ducks, but they are scarce ... I hear that my little sweetheart Ellen McGhie is engaged to be married. It seems strange to me, for I only remember her as a little girl, but the years have rolled along at their usual pace, and I suppose she has become a woman, though it seems just like the other day that we used to be good chums together. I wonder when I'll come across a girl that will marry me; still more do I wonder when I'll ever be in a position to take to myself a wife. Most of all do I wonder when I'll want to marry at all. I'm afraid we are in for a life of single blessedness, you and I.'

Jack had a contradictory temperament. He was then, and remained, of a solitary disposition. The lonely places of the world fascinated him, and he could probably never have settled down to a humdrum domesticated life in England. He was essentially a 'man's man'. He had none of the social graces, and, though attractive to women, his shy, gruff manner made it difficult for him to become intimate with the few he met. Yet another side of him longed for companionship, for the comforts of home life and a happy marriage. He never married and, if he had done so, perhaps he would soon have regretted his loss of freedom and felt again the call of the open spaces. There is something rather pathetic in this constant conflict between the two sides of his nature. A year or two later he again confided to Emily his longing for conjugal happiness:

'I would like to have a girl for a wife who looked something like Ellen ... I think I never saw a face I liked so well ... I think between you and me that I am a little bit sorry that "little Ellen" is married, though I am sure she is better off than ever she would have been with me.'

Nevertheless, he did not really regret his choice of a solitary life:

'I have not made my fortune, indeed I am poorer in everything but experience, still I do not regret the time spent in this country, taking one thing with another.'

He continued:

'I am writing this at 1.45 am., being compelled to sit up the best part of the night "on guard", for we have a prisoner in the "jug", one of our fellows who drank too freely and has been sentenced to 28 days … I have not been inside a church for three years. The nearest that I know of to here is 65 miles, too far to walk or ride. I do not emphasise this fact when writing to Alnwick, or the aunts would have a missionary dispatched forthwith. Of course they and folks at home have a vague notion that I have not many advantages of that sort, but I think if I were to state the bald fact that I have not seen a church interior for three years they would be horrified. I do not know if I am any the worse for this. I never was much struck on churches, Presbyterian at any rate. I suppose the wide prairie is as good a church, after all, as a Presbyterian barn or a Biblical picture gallery like your German church as described so graphically in your last letter.'

In 1896 gold was discovered in the Yukon, and the rush to Klondike began. With every man out for himself, it inevitably led to disorder and violence, and large forces of the 'Mounties' were needed to deal with the situation. Jack wondered how long it would be before he joined them:

'Our minds are more occupied at present with the Yukon than with anything else,' he wrote in February 1898. *'Several of our men have left our division this last month … and a special dispatch came yesterday warning every man <u>without exception</u> to be prepared to leave for the Yukon at an early date …so we are all wondering what a day may bring forth, and who may be the next to exchange the comparative comfort of a Line detachment and the fine winter climate of Alberta for the hardships of the Chilcoot Pass and the regions of the Arctic … Our number at the Ridge is three souls, and as the Corp. does not cook, Saxton and I have to take week about in the kitchen. If there is one duty I detest it is cooking, unless it happens to be during very stormy weather. If we go to the Klondike we may take a different view of the matter and look on cooking as a "snap", both on account of the welcome proximity of the stove when the thermometer registers 70 degrees below, and the exceeding simplicity of the bill of fare. I suppose those old stand-bys, pork and beans, will be the*

staple commodities – a great change from beef, mutton, antelope and chicken, all of which we have had here this winter, not to mention such delicacies as dried fruits, cheese, jam and pickles – and fresh eggs from our own hens and milk from our own cow.'

Jack, however, was not sent to the Yukon, no doubt to the great relief of his gastronomic soul.

North West Mounted Police capbadge
Courtesy www.rcmpolice.ca

CHAPTER VII

HOSPITAL AT LAST

'In the lowly air of Seven Dials'
W.S.Gilbert: Iolanthe

After Jack's departure Will moved into lodgings at Stockwell, and frequently walked all the way to the City and back to save the few pence needed for a tram fare, but in spite of all his economy it was nine years before he could begin his medical training. It would have been even longer had it not been for a loan from the ever-generous Aunt Ann, which he later repaid. He was twenty-six when, in 1889, he was at last enrolled as a student at Charing Cross Hospital. It had been a long and arduous struggle, but one which he was never to regret.

Will was a keen photographer. As early as 1887 he had sent fifty photographs to his parents, which Aunt Ann described as 'beautiful work,' and while at Charing Cross he took several pictures of the wards and operating theatre, which throw an interesting light on the conditions then existing in a London teaching hospital. In the centre of a typical ward there is a long table or chest of drawers covered with a fringed cloth. At one end stands a china jug and basin, and most of the rest of the table is taken up with aspidistras and other plants. A brass oil lamp hangs from the ceiling. Over the door is a framed text, and the walls are decorated with large pictures, mostly of Biblical subjects.

The nurses' uniform has leg of mutton sleeves with starched cuffs and high stiff collars, their voluminous skirts sweep the floor, their aprons are nearly as long, and their starched caps are tied under their chins with large stiff bows. The young doctors wear dark suits: no white coats in the wards in those days. In a photograph of the operating theatre the anaesthetist has gone so far as to remove his jacket and roll up his short sleeves, and the surgeon and his assistants are wearing gowns, but no one has a mask or even gloves. (A consultant – who always came to the hospital in a frock coat and top hat – would keep one of his old discarded coats in the theatre, bloodstained and green with age, especially for use at operations). The photograph shows a wooden table for the victim, a number of lights suspended from the ceiling and a festoon of dangling cords. Against the wall is a marble-topped piece of furniture with two sunken basins. Antisepsis was still in its infancy, and during Will's years at Charing Cross the carbolic spray, introduced by Joseph Lister many years before, was still occasionally used for disinfection.

In the early 1890s the district round Charing Cross contained some of the roughest elements in London, particularly in the vicinity of the then notorious Seven Dials. Here policemen always walked in pairs, and even the medical students – never noted for pusillanimity – hesitated to go there alone at night. Drunkenness was rife, violence all too common, and on Saturday nights the doctors on duty in the Casualty Department could expect several victims of brawls, often moribund or dead. 'Another stiff,' the porter would say, with a nonchalance bred of familiarity. 'Good,' might be the reply of the houseman on duty. This was less callous than it sounds; for a 'B.I.D.' (a patient brought in dead) he would receive a small but welcome fee for the examination of the cadaver and attendance at the autopsy, whereas if the patient died after admission he received no remuneration.

Will had a very successful student career, winning the two most important medical scholarships (the Llewellyn and the Golding) and gaining medals for Surgery, Senior Anatomy and Materia Medica. He qualified in 1894 and received a letter of congratulation from his father. 'May you, my dear fellow, long be spared to adorn our noble profession, and much success may you have in it, is my earnest prayer to our kind Heavenly Father.'

Will stayed on at Charing Cross as House Physician to Dr. Abercrombie and Demonstrator in Materia Medica. At this time diphtheria was as common as measles, and so great was the number of cases admitted to hospital that they could not be isolated, and they were frequently fatal. One day Dr. Abercrombie told his young House Physician that he wanted to try the new treatment that was being advocated by Joseph Lister. There might be nothing in it, but at least, he thought, it was worth trying. 'Would you like to come with me to see Lister?' he asked. Needless to say Will jumped at the chance of meeting the famous surgeon, and the two of them took a hansom cab and called on Lister, from whom they obtained the first diphtheria antitoxin to be used in Charing Cross Hospital. It was Will who had the privilege of demonstrating its use to the students, and he was always happy that, in his very humble capacity, he had participated in pioneering this far-reaching venture. He had a great admiration for the man who was largely responsible for it, and some years later (in 1902) he cut out a photograph of Lord Lister from the <u>British Medical Journal</u> and asked the great man to sign it – which he did. The surgeon's benevolent face looks down on me as I write.

Seven Dials, London circa 1900. Courtesy Chetham's Library, Manchester

Chapter VIII

LAND OF SAUERKRAUT AND LAGER BEER

'I will into some far countrey,
Where no man doth me know'
The Bailiff's Daughter of Islington

While Will was pursuing his medical studies and Jack was in Canada, their brother and sisters were one by one leaving home. When her school days were over Emily stayed at home for a little while, but William was, as always, hard up, and his eldest daughter felt that she should be doing something to ease the financial situation. Like her mother, she had little choice of profession and became a governess. Her first post was at Shawdon Hall, not far from Glanton, where she taught the two little Pawson boys, sons of the unfortunate gentleman whose wife had been burnt during the Jubilee celebrations. The following year she was teaching a little boy called George Leather at Fowberry Tower, near Wooler, and, as this was too far for even the sturdy Emily to walk every day, she stayed at Fowberry during the week and went home at weekends, weather permitting. On more than one occasion Fowberry was snowed up and Emily could not get home, but the weather did not keep her indoors. She took little George for long walks in deep snow, to the consternation of his mother, who feared for her child's health, but George approved of his stalwart young governess. Emily next went to Titlington, and this entailed a daily walk of five to six miles, but that did not worry her. She was still game for a five-mile walk when she was eighty.

Emily

50

For the next three years she stayed at home, giving lessons to her two youngest brothers. Alfred and Conrad attended the village school, which had been opened in 1875, but it was largely due to their sister's coaching that they eventually qualified for entrance to Alnwick Grammar School.

But by this time Emily was becoming restless. She was adventurous by nature. And, much as she loved Glanton, she longed to see something of the world. She had a flair for languages, and aspired to be a teacher of French and German rather than an ordinary governess, so she made up her mind to go to Germany. One day in November 1892, she went to Alnwick and had an advertisement translated into German for insertion in a German paper, at a cost of four shillings. She stayed overnight with her aunts. William told Clara, "walking each way in very dirty roads, for after frost we have had dark gloomy weather and of course bad roads." To back up the advertisement Emily had an excellent testimonial from Dr.Dungate, the principal of Alnwick Grammar School:

> *"Miss Robertson….. is a lady who has received a liberal education and whose accomplishments are of a high order….. she has also given evidence of being an excellent teacher. For three years Miss Robertson acted as governess to her two brothers and prepared them for entrance into The Alnwick Grammar School. They were able to take a good position in a higher form, and in the subjects of English, French, Latin and Mathematics, they have shown distinctly the results of a very thorough and rational teaching. These augur well for future success in school and College, and show that their first teacher is a lady who may take any educational position which she herself feels competent to fill."*

At first the advertisement met with no response, and Emily became very depressed – so much so that her young sister Ina found her difficult to live with. An ambulance class had been arranged in the village, and 'you know how anxious Em was to go when it was first talked of,' Ina wrote to Clara. 'Well, tonight she was as glum as possible because she had got this ticket given her and so had to go. I do not like saying anything about Em, but I do wish she had a pleasanter temper and would look pleased occasionally, it is very depressing living beside her.' Eventually, however, Emily was offered a post by a Frau Eiffler, who kept a small and select finishing school in Friedeberg, and her spirits revived. There was now a frantic rush to prepare her wardrobe, and her mother was kept very busy.

> *'I finished her summer grey dress,'* Elizabeth wrote to Clara.
> *'Today I am beginning the velveteen bodice, and then there will
> only be a few small things to do..........Florence has got us such
> a nice jacket for Em........it is nicely lined, has a nice black fur
> collar and a very good cloth.....only 15/6.'*

It was about this time that an attempt was made to re-introduce the
crinolene, and Ina wrote scornfully to Clara, 'What an awful fuss people
are making about the crinolene, the papers have articles about it every day.
There seems little fear of them coming just at present, I think.' Ina was
right; public opinion condemned it, a 'no-crinolene league' was formed,
and it never returned – fortunately for Elizabeth and her dressmaking.

In February 1893, Emily set out on her travels. Just before leaving she
received a short note from Will:

> *Just a line to wish you luck and prosperity on the land of
> Sauerkraut and Lager Beer ....I can't write much of a letter,
> having nothing on my brain but Hearts, Lungs and operations,
> etc.'*

Elizabeth accompanied Emily to Newcastle, where she embarked
for Hamburg. William had a letter from his wife describing Emily's
departure, and passed on the news to Clara:

> *'The boat did not get off till near 2 o'clock in the afternoon instead
> of 11 a.m. The Stewardess is a very nice woman and both she
> and the Captain said they would do everything to make Emily
> comfortable and also the Captain said that if Em did not travel
> till the following night......she might make the steamer her
> home all day instead of going to a hotel in Hamburg. Also that
> he would see to her getting comfortably off by Rail or at least see
> her to the Station. Emily was in fairly good spirits at parting.'*

As it turned out the Captain's services were not required in Hamburg.

To the present generation of young people it might seem that an unnecessary fuss was made of what, to them, is a commonplace. Emily was, after all, twenty-five. But eighty years ago things were very different. There was no easy travel, and young people were not as independent as they are nowadays. Emily had led a sheltered life; she had seldom been away from home except during her school days in London, and then she had Clara for company. Now she would be quite alone in a foreign land, living with people she had never met and of whose language she had only the scanty knowledge acquired at school. At first, however, she revelled in the excitement of the journey.

> *'The first few hours I enjoyed greatly,'* she wrote to her father. *'The sea was so beautiful and there was a delightful sense of freedom to be in the middle of it, without a ship or glimpse of land. The Captain kindly asked me up on the bridge with him, and I sat there for an hour or two. By and by, however, I began to feel rather queer, and disappeared below, where I remained some time, paying tribute to Father Neptune at intervals. By bedtime I was all right again.'*

The <u>Admiral</u> was evidently a very small ship, for there was only one other passenger, 'a young gentleman going to Danzig.' When they reached Hamburg, this gentleman, a Mr More, took Emily under his wing. He saw her through customs, took her on a tour of the town, then to the Streits Hotel, where she wrote postcards. This duty done, Mr More, took her to a restaurant for coffee, after which they went to a concert together. It would appear that the young man took quite a fancy to young Emily. In the evening he escorted her to the station, bought her ticket, wrote down all the changes she had to make, and left her in charge of a porter. 'Of course I insisted on paying myself for tea, trains, concert, etc.,' she wrote to her father, 'and he was gentleman enough to let me when he saw that I really meant it, so I hope that you do not think I did any harm going about with him. It was just downright kindness on his part, and I was very grateful to him, for I felt awfully queer and lonely.'

Did William and Elizabeth have some misgivings when they read this? In the 1890s it was not usual for well-bred young ladies to wander round foreign cities, unchaperoned, with strange men. Probably, however, they trusted Emily's good sense, and Elizabeth's reply to this letter made no reference to her daughter's spree with Mr More.

As soon as she arrived in Friedeberg, Emily sent her parents a vivid account of her journey after leaving Hamburg:

'The Night carriages to Berlin are splendid, just like our first class. They have lavatory affixed and the cushions pull down to form a couch, but they are fearfully heated. I was nearly ill with the heat, and could not get the window open. My fellow traveller – a German officer – was snoring away, so he was no good. The day carriages (2nd class) are very like our own, only without cushions. When I got to Berlin I had to change to the next station. The aforesaid officer kindly came to my help and as he spoke a little English told the porter what I wanted, and saw me into the bus, and made three very polite bows on leaving. I had two hours to wait at the other station, and then I started for Gorlitz……… Here the station officer made a tremendous fuss. I have not yet the slightest idea what he meant. I simply asked for a ticket. Here again, two kindly German women came to my help; but they could not speak a word of English. Anyway they took my part and got my ticket for me, and helped me about the money. I had not enough small change, and I think the man intended to cheat me, from what I could gather. Anyway it all got right in the end. I managed to explain what I wanted. Up to now I had felt wonderful, but now I was getting dreadfully tired and homesick. As long as the man raged it wasn't so bad, but when the two good Fraus began to pat me and tell me to "bekomen" (be comforted) and at last one of them pushed a large roll with a thick slice of red sausage into my hand, it was awful. It was all so absurd. The man raging at me, and one woman at him and the awful red sausage, that I could not help laughing nearly into hysterics, though all the time I felt like crying….When I got here there was no one at the station…..Madam Eiffler seems the soul of kindness…….I was very silly, and the first thing I did was just to be as miserable as ever I could, and desperate thoughts of taking the next train home rushed through my brain, so Madam kindly left me alone and sent Miss Thomas to help me…….Miss Thomas was so kind……. She brought me in a cup of coffee and roll, and helped me to unpack, and was so kind and cheery……… There *are only 6 boarders and 14 day scholars…..There are no fireplaces, only long close ware stoves going right up to the ceiling…..For dinner today we had soup…..it was rather funny stuff, and fried liver and potatoes. For breakfast and tea there are rolls and coffee, and for supper some sort of porter. Tea was made in my honour last night, brought in <u>glasses</u> and no milk in it. I thought it was hot beer, so did not take any.'*

Emily soon recovered from her homesickness, and settled in happily into her new surroundings – nor did it take her long, apparently, to acquire a taste for beer.

'I think I shall like my life here very much indeed. I think the school would compare very favourably with most English schools and is far away better than most continentals. The meat is very good. I will tell you the routine. We get up at 7 o/c and at half past have a roll and coffee. Such nice little rolls, new and warm. No butter, but they are made with milk and very slightly sweetened. The coffee is very good. Then we make our own beds, and classes begin at 8 o/c. At 11 there is bread and butter for those who wish. It is a kind of brown bread; I think there must be leaven in it. I do not much care for it, but I think people get to like it. It isn't bad. We get butter to the bread but not to the rolls. The butter is very good. Then for dinner there is always soup. That I like least. They use so much <u>vinegar</u> and <u>sugar</u> in their soups, but often it is very nice. After soup we have meat, mostly stews etc., not joints. I like the meat very much. It is brought cut into pieces on a large plate and passed round that we may help ourselves – with our own forks! No puddings as yet. Everything is clean and nice. After dinner classes and walking, and at 4 coffee and rolls again. Supper at half seven brown bread and butter, and meat of some kind, Bologna sausage or anything of the kind, and sometimes soup. Tonight we had fried potatoes, and Dutch cheese. Then after supper we have a glass of beer. "Einfach Bier" it is called – "simple beer" – very refreshing…….We have no strict clockwork discipline as in most schools. Most of the boarders are grown ups. Some pupil teachers, some help with the cooking, and so on……I have just begun to get into the ways of the classes. It is rather difficult at present, for my ear is not yet accustomed to

the strange sounds, and when they talk it is very like being in the parrot house in the Zoo. Then all my French lessons in Fr or German, so it is not very easy, but a good way to learn.'

Emily went on to describe her first impressions of Friedeberg. It was February, and there was deep snow, so she had not yet been far afield, but she was fascinated by the German houses, with their flat roofs, double windows and gaily coloured shutters. 'Green is the favourite colour. They all look as if they had been pitched out of a wheelbarrow.' She liked Frau Eiffler very much, but was not greatly attracted to her husband. 'Herr Eiffler is a strange looking mortal. He has longish hair and very red cheeks, and a voice like a raven.' She shared a room with two mistresses, and was amused by the German-style beds. 'We sleep on <u>down</u> beds, and over us we have a sheet and another down bed, no blankets.' Stoves warmed the rooms, and Emily missed the English coal fire. 'Never a blink of a fire except on my candle have I seen since I left the ship, and that is awful for a born stoker as I am!!"

England, too, was having severe wintry weather. Elizabeth's first letter to Emily told her of ten inches of snow at Glanton, so that the two youngest boys had been unable to go to school. As there was now a railway to Alnwick, they could attend as dayboys and did not have to endure the rigours of the aunts' house from which their elder brothers had suffered. But Glanton was three quarters of a mile from the station, and in a severe winter the road became impassable. Elizabeth was quite glad to have the boys at home. 'Very useful we found them, for what with the drifting, and such a quantity falling from the roof, we were pretty well blocked up.'

Emily's letter told of a concert she had attended:

'It only cost a few pfennigs but was quite a swell affair. We all went hatless and be gloved.....The performers were all in evening dress, great swells...... The girls in white, satin many of them, some pale blue and pink bodices, wide sashes and full sleeves and low necks, with flowers in their hair, quite a pretty sight..... I enjoy the music on Sundays very much.........Many German songs are very beautiful. The girls all take their needlework and sit and work. It seems strange to English ideas, but they are very

56

good people, and spend Sunday much better than many who think such work wrong.'

No one would dream of sewing or knitting at Glanton House on a Sunday.

With her usual zest for life, Emily enjoyed all the strange sights of a foreign town, even a funeral:

'Here it is a really comical sight. In front a boy goes with a cross all draped in black. Then follows a sort of German arrangement, the trumpeters in top hats, and with large bright-coloured bouquets in their buttonholes. The coffin is carried by young men, and, bringing up the rear, are all the women in the countryside, walking in twos, and dressed in their best and brightest clothes, with huge umbrellas or gay parasols, and all talking and laughing as if they were going to a wedding.'

In March, when she had spent a month in Frau Eiffler's household, Emily was still finding the culinary arrangements rather odd;

'We have just finished supper, and I am sitting with my glass of <u>beer</u> before me – deep in my cups! On the other side of the table is a plate of <u>raw beef</u>. How horrified you would all look if you saw it. I am getting quite accustomed to it – that is, the look of it, but I have not got to the eating stage yet! The variety in soups is quite amazing. I should think I have had 20 or 30 different sorts. They are quite an excitement, for you never know what a spoonful may bring forth. Mayhap a spoonful of <u>currants</u>, or <u>raisins</u>, followed by a stick of cinnamon, or perhaps some funny vegetables cut into shapes of A, B, C, or stars and flowers. It is like a "penny dip" in a brantub......So here you may fish up anything from a raw fish to a bird's nest. We <u>don't</u> but we <u>might</u> ....Did I tell you that one day we had "blauberry" soup? It was really our blauberries stewed with sugar, very nice, but they served it in a tureen, called it "soup," and we had it before meat...... Sour kraut is <u>awful</u>, a pig wouldn't eat it, I don't think even a <u>hen</u> – with <u>any</u> self-respect – would.'

In reply to an enquiry from Elizabeth, Emily described some of the pupils:

> 'The day scholars are a mixed set, all very "respectable" but plain folks, most of them. The boarders are very nice. Among the younger ones there is Lenie Wunsche. She is the daughter of quite wealthy people.........Johanna Braun is a pastor's daughter a village or two away. Fraulein Pfau is the daughter of a Dr. so _she_ is all right. Fraulein Bobertz is a young lady who is engaged to a Prof. of I don't know how many ics and ologies, and she has come to improve herself in some branches of literature and also domestic work. She helps in the cooking etc.'

CHAPTER IX

FESTIVALS AND FUNGI

'She took and gave language just
As she neede'
Matthew Frier: Jinny the Just

Emily had been in Friedeburg for only three or four months when she was faced with a problem. The school was losing money, and Frau Eiffler announced that she would be closing it in the following October. She offered to take Emily with her whenever she went, but Emily felt that by then she should be speaking the language fluently enough to look for a situation as an English governess. She soon found, however, that finding such a post was not going to be as easy as she had hoped. She spent a considerable sum of money on advertising, but without success. There were all too many English ladies in Germany wanting similar posts, many of whom were willing to give their services free for the sake of experience, or even to pay for the privilege. This Emily could not afford to do. At last, in the late summer, she received a letter from a Frau Kaskel in Bromberg, offering her a post on mutual terms in her pension, a boarding establishment for girls of a good family who were attending schools in the town. It was not what Emily had in mind, but time was passing and soon the school in Friedeburg would be closing, so she decided to accept Frau Kaskel's offer, if only as a temporary measure. She had to make up her mind in a hurry, and only five days later she said farewell to Frau Eiffler and set off for Posen. Though the distance was not very great, it was a complicated journey with seven changes, but by now Emily was quite capable of coping with irate-booking clerks or any other difficulties that might arise. 'I managed without a hitch,' she wrote, 'and feel quite proud of my achievement.'

Her decision proved to be the right one. As a governess she would have been expected to speak English all the time, whereas at the pension she had to speak German and had lessons from Frau Kaskel. In return, she helped in the house in the mornings, feeding the canary, watering the plants and filling the lamps. In the afternoons she superintended the pupils and talked with them.

'After dinner,' she wrote, 'I take the girls out for a walk. This is
the worst bit and I always feel quite thankful I get them safely

59

home again without a duel or an elopement. Several of them are very pretty girls, and the officers and "boys" are always on the watch. I have to watch and plan to take them different roads, and of course they also watch and plan, so it is not always just so easy to do what is best, and as the girls are mostly grown up one cannot just treat them like children.'

In Bromberg Emily was still faced with unusual meals:

'The great dish at the present is mushrooms, or rather toadstools, for nothing more or less were the unrighteous looking things which are eaten........The fungus hunt generally took place in the dusk The pursuit was of a melancholy nature. They went about with sticks furtively turning over the dead leaves as though expecting and yet dreading to find the remains of a corpse underneath. Every now and then they would pick up a mouldy-looking thing, smell it, and put it into their bag. In vain might the toadstool protest, in vain assume the most odious shapes, venomous colours, and reptilian blotches, in vain exhale the most objectionable odours, and smell at the top of its voice till one could hear it smelling a mile off. They wouldn't believe it, not even upon its oath, and away it went to the bag and finally into the soup. But it is melancholy feeding at best, this s(o)up full of horrors. No one ever asks for a second help. It was a sufficient achievement to get rid of one lot without a casualty. They inform each other that such a mushroom is very like, indeed almost impossible to distinguish from one of the most deadly species known, in fact only really to be discovered – by results. The company turns pale, but only remarks that it is "curious" and takes a glass of beer. The conversation turns upon remedies for fungus poisoning, and the inefficiency thereof, and all look out for the first symptoms of an attack........There are many kinds in the market. They stew them up with pepper, salt, butter and herbs, and they have a very agreeable flavour of pepper, salt, butter and herbs.'

Emily's light duties allowed her plenty of leisure, and she began to seek private pupils. At the beginning of September the first of these arrived. 'She is to have two lessons a week, of 2 hours each, and pays 1/- an hour, so that....will keep me from begging.' A fortnight later she had two more pupils – a Frau Goetsch and a Herr Barwald, a Jewish lawyer. The latter caused her considerable amusement.

> '*You should see how the German people write letters. They <u>are</u> polite! The other day I had a note from Herr Barwald, just a few lines to say he couldn't come for English, but My Word! I got quite a fright. I thought I was the Kaiserin, for it was addressed to the "Hochwohlgeboren" literally "The high well born" and inside it began with "Sahrgeehrtes" (greatly venerated) and ended with his "most excellent high esteem." Of course it doesn't mean so much in German, but that is the <u>literal </u>translation…… I didn't venture an answer in German, I'm not well enough up in my adjectives, so contented myself with plain Eng. "Dear Mr B." and "Yours truly".*'

Emily still missed the good old English open fire:

> '*We sat yesterday actually with a fire, the first time this season. By fire, of course, I mean the oven. A real fire I have never seen since I left England. There is not a spark or even glow to be seen, but they warm the room very well. I am now accustomed to the fireless carpet less rooms in Germany. In Germany the rooms are as a rule very large, and the floors painted light brown and then finely polished, and here and there a square of carpet or a rug. They look very roomy and clean, but I prefer ours, and oh for a fire to poke,*'

Sometimes she visited the local market with Frau Kaskel.

> '*The Mart is a large square, and all the people come from the surrounding country with their wares. It is a very picturesque sight to see all the country folk in bright-coloured aprons and headgear sitting round with all sorts of articles beside them. The people who buy have nearly all sort of pokes of network string, and herein goes every mortal thing. At the bottom, perhaps, a live duck, then a few handfuls of mushrooms, next a lot of pears and plums. A cucumber and a vegetable narrow stick up above, and all the corners are filled up by a pint or two of blueberries or cranberries poured in promiscuously. The fruit is very fine*

this year but in some places the selling of it has been forbidden on account of the cholera. Here we drink boiled water just for a precaution.'

There was cholera in England, too, at this time, as mentioned in a letter to Emily from Alfred.

It was Emily's wish to improve her French as well as her German, and, if possible, to find a post in France later on. With this in view she began taking lessons in French with a young German woman called Olga, and a close friendship grew up between the two girls. Though after Emily left Bromberg they met only once, nineteen years later, they corresponded regularly until the outbreak of the First World War. It grieved Emily that she could never discover what had happened to her old friend.

She now had several pupils, including a young merchant of twenty who was hoping to visit England on business. The lawyer, Herr Barwald, was still coming to her regularly, and now that she had overcome her initial shyness in teaching a middle-aged man she enjoyed their sessions together. They were reading Macaulay's Essays and German history, 'and if he does unmercifully murder the Queen's English and I do not just speak "German as she is spoke," why 'taint no matter anyhow!'

William and Elizabeth must have rejoiced when the postman brought them a letter from Emily. Neither of them had ever been abroad, and their eldest daughter's breezy accounts of her doings and of the German people gave them a glimpse of a life very different from their own quiet existence at Glanton.

'Sunday was a grand day here,' she wrote in September, 1893, *'A fine monument was unveiled. It is an equestrian statue of Kaiser Wilhelm I. The Kaiser could not come, but some great guns in the form of Archdukes, Counts and Grafs, came in his stead. The town was decorated and illuminated, and there was a wonderful procession, which lasted 2 or 3 hours. We had 2 windows so had a fine view of the whole affair. The procession was very interesting. It was composed of representatives of all the trades in Bromberg and the surrounding towns. Every group was heralded by a detachment of soldiers and band of music. First*

came a lot of the black-coated, top-hatted gentry, the "Berhorden" (that is all the public "characters" from the Burgermeister down to the "Bum"). Then there were the butchers, all in pink blouses and round black caps and white aprons. The bakers, in white, with white caps and blue silk scarves over the soldier, and tiny strings of _buns_ round their caps. The chimney sweeps, in black velvet, and carrying their brushes and ladders wreathed with flowers. The blacksmiths with long black beards – typical of blacksmiths for some reason or another – the "Fursters" (they are sort of gamekeepers, but much higher than our gamekeepers. The upper Fursten are quite gentlemen). They are always dressed in light (Lincoln?) green and look very pretty. Then there was a great crowd of all the trades, mixed up but each carrying a sign of his industry, the house-painter his palette, tailor his shears, the basket-maker a lovely basket filled with flowers, the bargemen with a little boat, railwayman with his signal post, the watchman with his horn lantern and little dog, and a whole host of men in the machinery department with pots and pans, engines, sewing machines and everything you can think of. All in miniature, hoisted on poles and wreathed with flowers. It was very pretty and uncommon. Everything went off well. The Germans are all kept in order, and, like very good people, are just a little uninteresting. Of course it is very nice to see such an orderly crowd and to meet no drunk men, and so on, and quiet is very dear to my soul, but still I wished for once they would _shout_ a bit more. There seemed a want of enthusiasm somehow. Once they got up a "Hoch" (our hurrah) but only those who took part in the procession, and of course they sang "The Watch on the Rhine" and when they sang the National Anthem (same tune as ours) I felt for a moment I was in England again, and jumped to my feet to join in the chorus, but even then the crowd didn't join. Why, in Eng. every man, woman and child is up in the air with hat off directly, but here not. Perhaps they were afraid of committing that most unpardonable sin "Majestate Beleidigung", which is that should you make a remark to the effect that his most unserene Majesty has a hole in his stocking or a weakness for sausages (not to say Schnapps), you are liable to a month in prison. It is quite true. Here one must be quite particular what one says. Just lately a lady of position was over heard on the street to say to a friend *that the Empress Augusta wore a wax neck, and was pulled up for "Majestate Beleidigung" and got free lodgings for a fortnight, and another who made some rather personal remarks as to his appearance got a month. I like to tease them. On Sunday I saw a bust of his Majesty, which was hoisted on a pole, and all "G.J.". I said he was evidently fond of his Schnapps and looked very jolly, not to say "betrunken," and was at once informed that I must not say so, or at least not on the street, as it was a "Majestate Beleidigung." It is very comical. And now for a little more redtapeism. I have been told today officially to write to Papa and ask him for a paper stating that I am here for the purpose of learning German (do not do any teaching) and that I came with full permission from my parents <u>and</u> the <u>Magestrate</u> and it must be written and signed by the said Magestrate and sent in a week, or else I shall be bundled out of Germany and sent back to you – a very pleasant arrangement, but one which would not suit my present plans.'*

A little later Emily had another unexpected treat:

'Last week I was at a lovely concert. It cost 3/- and of course was quite beyond me. Fr. Kaskel was going with some of the older girls. However, a friend of hers came [and she could not go,] and of course someone of mature age, homely features and severe disciplinary manners must go with the girls to watch over them and ward off the dreadful "military men" and such like characters, so, as I was most fit to fill this responsible post, I got Fr. Kaskel's ticket to my great delight......It was a great treat........Last evening I was invited out to my first "kaffee" party........They are really just "afternoon teas" where a number of ladies meet together to discuss – the affairs of the nation, of course, and drink kaffee and eat a great many cakes. But no gentlemen are admitted to our sacred conclaves. They might see how interestingly small appetites expand on such occasions.........They are very jolly little parties......We talked and had a little music and played games.........The Fräuleins Greidrich are very nice. The eldest, Olga, gave me French lessons........The prejudice against Jews is very strong here. Even in school the Jewish children have rather a bad time........Here we are just on the borders of Poland and

only two hours from Russia. Nearly all the peasants speak Polish – when they dare – but many of their masters will not allow it. Poland, I suppose, is no longer a free country, and the people must identify themselves with the people of the country where they live. It is not considered wise "politically" for them to have their own language and customs any more. I suppose there is a danger that they may rouse up to patriotism once more...... Their chains do not seem to trouble them, more pity. Yet there were once heroes amongst them, and why not again?.... At the Kaffee I wore my velvet blouse and everyone is delighted with the great sleeves and large collar.'

Emily, once the tomboy who cared nothing about clothes, was becoming quite fashion conscious:

'I have bought a nice little fur cap..........It cost 6/6. It is just a soft toque, black fur on top, and beaver round about (real tho'). The two colours match my jacket, which has black fur, and my muff which is brown.'

Her mother, too, realised that Emily's gay social life called for smarter clothes than she had taken with her:

'If you think that pretty black dress with mauve silk lining would be of any use to you, I will send it to you. I only wore it once and the make with deep flounce is quite fashionable yet..... It would be nice for semi-dress.'

When Christmas approached Emily felt rather homesick. It had always been a very festive occasion at Glanton House, and this was the first time she had spent it away from home. All the family who were in England, scattered though they now were, made a point of going home for Christmas, even though for Will and Florence it meant travelling up from London by night on Christmas Eve and back on Boxing Night. Until 1893 only Jack, far away in Canada, had been absent, but now there was another gap at the Christmas table. A few days later Elizabeth wrote to Emily, telling her how they had spent the day. This time there had been one innovation of which, one feels, Elizabeth did not quite approve:

'We have had turkey instead of goose. Papa was at Abberwick one day, and there saw a fine flock of turkeys, so ordered one for Christmas. Strange to say your Uncle sent one too, so it has been "Turkey yesterday – Turkey today" etc. Both were to use for fear of spoiling, so we boiled the Newcastle one on Sunday. It caused no little amusement and anxiety, it was huge – 1and 1/2lbs – and would not go into the Fish Kettle, and was to boil in the furnace pot. Even there it was a tight fit, and the getting out was no joke.........On Monday we roasted the Abberwick one and it was very good, and so was the pudding. We will not taste goose this year – a thing I never remembered to have happened before. On Tuesday......we had a girdle cake.......We had not a grand spread at night – only fruit and cake and coffee.....Uncle sent the usual supply of raisins and figs and a nice book. The turkey instead of ginger and nuts etc...... The Berkeleys sent me a lovely cosy, green satin and plush.'

Emily stayed in Germany for more than two years, but her ambition of going on to France was, for some reason, not fulfilled, and she returned to England in June 1895. She apparently travelled from London to Newcastle by sea. 'Poor girl, what a voyage she had from London on that stormy night', wrote her Aunt Eliza, who saw her soon after her return. 'I thought her looking very pale and not strong.'

During the next few years Emily had various positions as governess in England. On one occasion, when teaching a very small boy the elements of religion, she tried to explain to him in simple terms the omnipresence of God. The little boy considered the matter deeply, then asked:

> 'Could God get into this room?'
> 'Oh yes,' Emily replied.
> 'Could He get under the table?'
> 'Er – yes.'
> 'Could He get under the tablecloth?'
> 'Well, yes He <u>could</u>.'

What else could Emily say? The small boy looked long at the table, then:

> 'My' he said in awe. 'God must be very <u>flat</u>.'

Another of her pupils was given to using grown-up words, whether or not she knew their meaning. She was also a very polite little girl. After having tea with some of her young friends and consuming large quantities of bread and jam and cream cakes and fruit jellies, she said good-bye very prettily to her hostess, adding demurely, 'Thank you for my very frugal tea.'

Emily was greatly loved by all her pupils, most of whom kept in touch with her long after they were grown up and had children of their own.

CHAPTER X

THE FAMILY IS SCATTERED

'Thy brood is flown'
Tennyson: The Princess

(i)

While Emily was in Germany, her next eldest sister Clara had also become a governess. In 1882 she went to a family in Harrogate, and at first was quite happy there. She liked her pupil, and was frequently taken for drives round the Yorkshire countryside, which she found very enjoyable. Her employers treated her kindly, and she hoped that she was settled there until her pupil reached school age.

Back in Glanton, her sisters regarded Harrogate as a metropolis, and gave Clara many shopping commissions, the most important being a twenty-first birthday present for Florence.

> 'If you can get a nice pendant and chain <u>and</u> a book for the money do,' Ina wrote. 'If not we think you should get the chain but we do not know what price they are likely to be..... If by making up two or three shillings more you could get both chain and book we will try to make it up and send it......it would be nice to get either Tennyson or the Album along with the chain, but I fear that will be impossible. If you have to get either Ten. or Album Papa would prefer the Album, <u>he</u> does not like Ten. at all. We think you might get a chain about 5/-.'

Poor Clara: History does not relate what she purchased as a result of this involved letter. Ina went on to tell her sister about the 'Hiring Day,' which was apparently at Glanton House:

> 'The Hiring day is over and gone once more and today we have the pleasant job of clearing up the dirt.'

Someone who had attended the hiring stayed for dinner:

> 'I do not think much of him, he is a goose and not a very

gentlemanly one either. The way he lolled on his chair and scraped his feet about and stuck his arms on the table: and he hardly ever spoke to Mamma, or Papa either very much during dinner. We had plum pudding which was very good, and tapioca was never touched.'

Hardly surprising, one would think!

There follows a rather cryptic remark:

'The Dental Dynamite was sent yesterday. That Dynamite is a fraud, those tiny bottles are only half full.'

There are several references to 'Dynamite' in letters from other members of the family. Was it some new kind of dentifrice?

It was at about this time that the fourteen-year-old Conrad, never a great correspondent, managed to write four pages to Clara. He was still at school, and his letter informed his sister that he had passed his geometry examination; but he was more interested in the Glanton House garden, where he and Alfred had spent much of their spare time as assistant gardeners. 'The garden is in an awful state just now, you can hardly see anything for weeds. We have been working in it at the rate of 1d an hour'.

The following year Clara was very unwell, and William prescribed a moderate amount of alcohol. 'I think claret and even a glass of port may do you good, taken however only so long as you seem to require it for I do not like these things much nor have I much faith in them.'

This was the year in which George, Prince of Wales (later King George V) married Princess Mary of Teck. 'Is anything going to be done in Harrogate in honour of the Royal Wedding?' Ina asked. 'Mrs Pawson of Shawdon Hall is going to give a picnic to the four schools with the parents and friends of the children and is preparing for 800 people.'

By this time Clara had become dissatisfied with her post. Though she was kindly treated, her employers were quite incapable of making up their minds about anything. They planned a holiday at Morecambe, then postponed it. They agreed on a date for Clara's annual holiday, but changed their minds at the last moment, and in Williams's opinion interfered too much with her work. 'Are you not badgered too much with your pupil?' he asked. 'Tell Mrs T. from me that you require more rest and quiet from worry before you can expect to improve or be able to continue with the family.' One wonders whether the shy and retiring Clara ever passed on her father's message. Her Aunt Ann also disapproved of her remaining at Harrogate, though for a different reason:

> 'It is very well in some respects, though not altogether the best thing for your own improvement, unless you are careful to make up for it by profitable reading and diligent study........To be making progress in the Divine life is of the first importance seeing that our time here is short and uncertain.'

This was written in June, 1893, and Clara left Harrogate in the following month, though whether her departure was due to her father's anxiety about her health, her aunt's concern for her moral welfare, or merely to please herself, we do not know. Emily, writing from Friedeburg, was delighted. 'They are a silly lot,' was her opinion. Just before Clara came home, young Ina exhorted her 'not to forget to bring all old shoes, corsets and gloves you have as they may come in useful if not too bad.'

After one or two temporary posts, Clara went in 1896 to Ireland where she settled down happily with the Glenny family. Here she took up cycling. 'So you are quite an expert cyclist,' wrote Elizabeth. 'I can imagine it to be splendid exercise ....Do you tumble often? I see accounts of many nasty accidents to ladies from falling off their "bykes". You must be careful and not too adventurous.' (In later years both Clara and Ina did have very nasty accidents through free-wheeling down the hill from Glanton with their feet on the handle bars, and forgetting that it was advisable to put on their brakes before reaching the cross-roads.) By the following year the new pastime had caught on in Glanton too. 'Cycling is quite the rage here as elsewhere,' wrote Elizabeth. 'It seems quite a disease. Fancy 5 cycles standing at Bessie Robson's door on a Sunday afternoon,' There was even a rumour that someone was to set up a bicycle-hiring establishment in Glanton in the summer.

'Have you no chance in this line?' William wrote to Emily.

'Soon we shall have horseless carriages, auto-motor cycles and everything of that sort, so we shall fly about the country without trouble or fatigue – but, I fear, not without expense!.....I see there is to be a Great Exhibition of all those sorts of things next month, both at the Imperial Institute and the Crystal Palace. I should like to be there. Even a flying machine model is to be included.'

While Clara was in Ireland she had an S.O.S. from Ina:

'Could you manage to spare a shilling or two to buy curtains for the staircase? The old ones are done and it looks so wretched without them. They will cost about 3/- or 3/6 but if you could even send 2/6 it would be a great help. Send it to me but don't make it payable to anyone and then it will just send away again and save 1d.'

Even allowing for the greater purchasing power of money in the 1890s Ina's appeal highlights the financial difficulties under which Elizabeth and William were still living, even though most of the family were now grown up. Their complaints about rising prices have a familiar ring over a hundred years later. When William was given a pair of gloves for his birthday, Elizabeth told Clara;

'He was much pleased with his gloves. As well he might, they are beautiful gloves – real reindeer, but a beautiful price. However, if all join it will be reasonable, 7/6. I never saw gloves that price before.'

In 1897 Queen Victoria celebrated her Diamond Jubilee, and again Glanton was to join in the national junketings.

'We are all excitement here about the Jubilee,' Elizabeth wrote to Clara. *'1887 was a grand affair but this will surpass it. As before, several of the surrounding places have asked to unite with us, and already 60 people have been gathered. The tea and sports are to be on the Hill, but the bonfire is to be on Titlington Mount, and Mrs Howard is doing it, excepting the Tar Barrels which Glanton will provide.....I wonder whether it is the outing or loyalty to the Queen that makes so many willing to give so*

71

*liberally! On Sunday – the real Accession Day – there is to be a
Service on the Hill, and all the Volunteers and Band and Choir
to take part in it.........It is Lipton, the Tea Merchant, who has
given the £25,000 to the Princess of Wales' fund.'*

Clara stayed in Ireland until 1901, after which she remained at Glanton
until the outbreak of the First World War.

Florence

(ii)

Florence, the middle girl, was in many ways unlike the rest of the family.
She was small, vivacious, like a perky little bird. She was, however, a
very determined person. She had no intention of becoming a governess
like her elder sisters. No, <u>she</u> was going to London to be a secretary. Her
parents did not quite approve. Girls did not work in offices in the 1890s;
that was a man's job, they said. But Florence was sure she could do the job
as well as any man, and to London she went. She had learned shorthand
and typing, but finding a job was not as easy as she had expected. There
was no lack of vacancies, but prejudice against women in commerce was
very strong – especially when the woman concerned was a girl in her
twenties. She could not possibly be as competent as a <u>man</u>; she would

have a disrupting influence on the junior clerks; and so on. Eventually she did obtain a post, but left hurriedly when she found that her middle-ages employer wanted her to be more to him than a secretary. So she was out of work, living in one room, with barely enough money to feed herself, and it seemed as if her parents were right; women secretaries were not wanted. Many girls would have given up, but not Florence. She persevered, and presently was given a trial by a Mr Cooper, who proved to be a kind and considerate employer. At first she was treated coldly by the rest of the all-male staff, but it was not long before her friendliness, her lively sense of humour and her undoubted competence overcame their prejudice, and she became a very popular member of staff. She soon proved her ability (we hear frequently of increases in her salary), and she stayed with Mr. Cooper for many years.

While Will was in London, he and Florence met frequently, and on one occasion he escorted her to a dance at the house of Mrs Barber. Florence sent Clara an account of it.

> '*The first thing I must tell you about is the Fancy Dress Dance......
> It was a great success and I think everyone enjoyed themselves. I
> was glad I went, but at the same time I don't care if I never go
> to another. There was a great variety of costumes and they looked
> very pretty. As I hardly danced at all I felt rather out of it. I was
> so glad Will was able to go, it made it much nicer for me. I had
> two dances with him....... I danced the Barn Dance with Mr
> Tidy. I couldn't do it a bit, didn't even know the steps.......I
> liked Will as Faust.......I wish I were able to dance, but at the
> same time I am not particularly gone on it. I expect I am getting
> too old, still it does make me feel a duffer.*'

Florence was just twenty two!

Even before Will had qualified, his young sister Marion had decided to become a nurse. She began her training in Edinburgh, but later followed her brother to Charing Cross. It was a hard life in those days. There were no ward maids, and the nurses had to carry out all the menial chores. Their sleeping quarters were austere, and they had little off-duty time. It was not until 1921 that the nurses at Charing Cross were given one full day off a week, thanks to the pertinacity of the then Matron. And there was certainly no financial inducement to join the profession; three years after Marion had begun her training William reported that she had received her first sovereign. But Marion never regretted her choice; she was a born nurse.

Marion

While at Charing Cross she fell in love with one of the doctors, and they became engaged. It seemed as if one, at least, of the Robertson girls was not destined to remain a spinster. But Marion, in spite of her Victorian upbringing, had many modern views, and she took up smoking – only in private, of course, and she did not indulge very often, but she enjoyed the occasional cigarette. Her fiancé objected; not on medical grounds, for lung cancer and other ills were not in those days associated with cigarette-smoking, but because he did not consider it ladylike. Most people in the 1890s would probably have agreed with him.

Though the time had passed when the gentlemen donned smoking jackets and retired to a special room if they wished to indulge in this unpleasant habit, for a woman to smoke was carrying emancipation too far. Even Marion's own family disapproved. Fifteen years later, when Florence went to London she was horrified to see women smoking in restaurants. 'Disgusting,' she said. But Marion saw no reason to give up her mild indulgence, and, since the doctor refused to withdraw his ban, she broke off her engagement. She made it clear that this was not because she could not give up smoking – she was no addict – but because she felt that, if he laid down the law over such a minor matter, he would expect to rule her life in more important issues. She did not intend to be ruled by anyone; he was not the husband for her. So ended the only serious romance in the lives of this quartet of spinsters.

When she had completed her training Marion went to a children's hospital in Manchester. Unfortunately, after about ten years, she developed pulmonary tuberculosis, and had to give up hospital work. The disease was tackled in time and she recovered, but she was advised to spend a few years in a warmer climate. A Dr. Taylor, a friend of the family, was setting up a clinic in Las Palmas, and Marion accompanied him and his wife as nurse. Her youngest sister, Ina, to whom she was devoted, visited her there, and Ina's gaiety and a pair of large and soulful eyes, made her very popular with the young men on the island.

(iii)

Alfred and Conrad left school in 1893, and Ina wrote to Emily:

'The boys' school days are over, and yesterday was prize giving day. Con got a very nice one, The Universe, so nicely bound. Poor Alf did not get any and he is awfully disappointed as he expected two and Con and all the other boys at school declare that he ought to have had the 1st Latin prize as he has been top in Latin far oftener than anyone else.'

Alfred

Clara had just left Harrogate, so during that summer she taught Alfred shorthand and book-keeping. He then found a job of some kind, but was evidently still living at home or near at hand, as William often mentioned his help in the garden and stables. Two years later Jack came home for a short holiday, and when he returned to Canada in 1896 he took Alfred with him. Clara had just gone to Ireland, and Elizabeth felt very sad at this further break-up in the family. 'It is a terrible ordeal. If I were not so busy, and had I time to think, I do not think I could go through with it.' She had another worry on her mind too. It seemed Jack was likely to become engaged before long to a girl of whom Elizabeth did not approve. 'I feel quite certain now, although I have not been told. It is horrid, but we must make the best of it, I suppose.' She need not have worried, for no more was heard of the affair, and the lady in question later married somebody else.

William felt Alfred's departure keenly. 'I miss him at every turn, especially at the stable, but I like now to do his work, which he did so long and so faithfully for me'. Of all the large family, Ina was now the only one still at home, and she did her best to take Alfred's place. 'Ina is now our treasure,' William wrote to Clara, 'and she helps me in the stable….I do miss dear Alf. He was always ready to go on errands and attend to poor Polly (the pony).'

Jack and Alfred had a miserable journey.

'They had a slow and rough passage,' Elizabeth told Clara, 'and were not sorry when that stage of their journey was near an end, especially Alf, who is not a good sailor and never was quite comfortable, and did not enjoy the voyage a bit…..The accommodation was not so good as Jack had expected on such a vessel.'

They were further upset by the death of a baby, who was buried at sea. The weather, too, was against them.

> *'It was intensely cold as they approached the shore, and I doubt they would come into the dreadful cold spell the newspapers have said so much about.'*

They did, and Alfred's nose was frozen – not a happy introduction to Canada.

Jack went on to a place with the delightful name of 'Writing on Stone,' where he re-joined his old detachment of the Mounties. Alfred went to the Young's farm, where Jack had spent his first year, and celebrated his arrival by contracting measles. He soon recovered, and Jack, who had had a letter from him, reported that he seemed to be in good spirits and working hard. Like all his family, Alfred was very fond of music, and no mean performer, and was pleased to find that Alec Young had an organ in his house. The news of Alfred's musical accomplishments soon spread, and he was in great demand. In 1898 he wrote to Emily:

> *I believe there is going to be another dancing party tomorrow night, so I will be in for lots of work, playing the organ......We are going to start a choir practice down at Humesville. They certainly need it, for the singing is horrible, and so slow....I have to give a music-lesson tonight.'*

In the following year Alfred left the Young's and went to Winnipeg, where he was to spend the rest of his short life. Here the winters were very severe, temperatures being often 40 to 50 degrees below zero, and frost-bitten noses and ears a common experience.

In Winnipeg Alfred attended a business college to fit himself for a career other than farming, which did not appeal to him, and after spending the summer in temporary jobs, he found a permanent clerical post in connection with the construction of a railway. He earned a pound a week, which his father thought 'not too bad.'

When Conrad left school he became an engineer. During his apprenticeship he was invited to join some friends on a short holiday in Glasgow if his father could afford it.

> *'Con is likely to have a trip with the Ainslies for four days at Easter,'* William wrote to Emily. *'At least, he would like it, and I suppose we must consent, though it will cost about a £1 railway and lodgings etc. at Glasgow...The railway fare is to be only 8/- there and back.'*

(iv)

Ina was the last of the family to leave home. As all her brothers and sisters were now earning their living, it was decided that she should stay at home with her mother. She and Elizabeth were certainly never idle. Even with most of the family away, there was plenty of work to do in Glanton House, and they had little help. The most dreadful event of the year, from the domestic point of view, was the annual 'cleanings,' when, for several weeks in the spring, the whole house was turned upside down. The upheaval caused by these 'cleanings' can hardly be visualised by the most house-proud of modern matrons. In this Victorian home every room was filled to overflowing with furniture, every inch of wall-space was occupied by pictures and ornamental plates, every table had its cloth. Fire-places were draped with curtains, dressing-tables and wash-stands had each their own sets of mats, grates were filled in the summer with crepe paper or rushes, and mantelshelves and cabinets overflowed with china ornaments and photographs.

Lavinia (Ina)

Every carpet had to be taken up and beaten in the yard. Every mat, every piece of china and glass, had to be washed. The heavy full-length window-curtains, and the long tapestry curtains draped round the beds, all had to be washed by hand in the copper. Floors had to be scoured, walls colour-washed. Feather beds were lugged outside, shaken, and hung on the hedge to air. The massive mahogany furniture was dragged out of each room in turn. Linen blinds were taken down, scrubbed and ironed. And all without the aid of any labour-saving device. Every Spring Elizabeth's letters contain references to this terrible ordeal. In April, 1896, for instance, she wrote to Clara:

> *'The week before last we got the kitchen thoroughly cleaned, ceiling and all, but oh dear! Mary is a slowcoach – it took her a whole day to colour the front kitchen, did not even get the entry done or the floor washed.....On Monday we did the spare bedroom......I have got new shades for the spare room, very inexpensive but very pretty, and a new butter muslin cover for the dressing-table, and the old room looks very respectable. On Thursday Ina and I set to work to take the dining room to pieces – we cleared it completely, and Mary came on Friday. Again it took her the whole day to do*

the bare room. She did scour the floor, but I did a good part of the painting. She does her work <u>well</u>, but is frightfully long about it, so on Saturday the carpet was to lay down and the room to put together again. Ina and I cleaned the furniture, curtain poles, etc. on Friday ready to lift in….. Em's room is cleaned, but I shall not put the bed curtains up yet, indeed they are not washed yet. We get on so slowly, because we cannot go at it all day, someone is sure to come in if we are not prepared in the afternoon, and with the ordinary housework to do, it gives little time for the cleaning.'

It would not have occurred to Elizabeth to say to an unexpected caller, as might a modern housewife, 'I'm sorry to be so untidy. We're in the middle of spring-cleaning.' Even to open the front door to a visitor while wearing her apron and 'dusting cap' would have been unthinkable. After lunch she must change into her black dress, don her lace cap, and be 'respectable.'

When not engaged in housework their hands were not idle. It is in 1898 that we find the first reference to 'vamps', and for the next year they are frequently mentioned in letters from both Ina and her mother. It would seem that these were shoe-vamps, in which the two women worked lace-holes for a small remuneration. Clara, too, had worked at them while she was at home.

'Your share for the Vamps,' Elizabeth told her, 'you did

4 prs plain holes – 4 ½ d per pair	-	1 – 6
2 prs round holes laced 6d	-	1 – 0
1 pr small holes laced 6d	-	6
		3 – 0'

A fortnight later Ina complained that vamps were few and far between. 'We don't take 2/6 a week at present. Once we had a pale heliotrope pair and a red, the rest are all black.' The heliotrope and the red sound very dashing! Ina mentioned that they had twelve pairs with lace stitch and six without. They evidently entailed a considerable amount of work for small reward – 'It is poor pay,' Elizabeth wrote, about 2d or sometimes 2½d per hour. Still we are glad of it.' They must have been very hard up indeed to work so industriously for such a pittance. Indeed, the following year William again talked of leaving Glanton because, 'this place does not yield enough to keep us, few as we are, and with all the economy we can practise. I fear I will before long be starved out altogether, and must look for some other situation where at least we could reduce our expenses.'

They did, however, find time for social life, and in 1899 Elizabeth told Clara of an evening devoted to the then fashionable pastime of table-turning:

> *'We persuaded the Thompsons [who lived at the Villa] to take a little supper with us....We tried the <u>table-talking</u> [sic], and with Flo as a medium it did capitally. I was glad, for you know it has been so often tried with the Thompsons and it would never answer. I think they were both rather excited about it, and a good deal <u>awed.</u>'*

Ina stayed at home until 1900, but in that year she had thrust upon her a job that she would certainly not have chosen for herself. Shortly before the turn of the century it had become clear that Elizabeth's brother Conrad, who was a widower living in Newcastle, could no longer live by himself. Ina, and some of her sisters when available, had previously stayed with him for short periods to help him, but he was not an easy man to live with, and they did not enjoy their visits. Now it became apparent that a more permanent arrangement must be made. Apart from sisterly concern for her only surviving brother, Elizabeth may have had another reason for wanting to help him. He was a wealthy man, and in 1900 William wrote to Emily;

> *'If your Uncle White comes up to his implied promise of assistance, I think we shall enjoy a little more pecuniary prosperity than it has been our fortune to share in times past.... I do not know whether you have heard that your Uncle is worth about £10,000 or £15,000?....To your Mother he indicated that all he possessed would revert to her and her dear Bairns....I feel often saddened that our girls should have had to undergo so many hardships and my own dear Emily the worst.'*

Elizabeth was the least mercenary of women, but she would have been less than human if she had not looked forward to an easing of the financial difficulties which had beset her and William throughout their married life. Perhaps too, there was a condition attached to Uncle Conrad's promise. Be that as it may, in 1900 Ina was despatched to Newcastle to look after her uncle <u>sine die</u>.

In spite of his difficult temperament, Conrad was very kind to Ina. She was certainly more fortunate than her Aunt Eliza, who had had such a dreary life with her hermit-like uncle, the wine merchant. Conrad had a country house at Rothbury, ten miles from Glanton, where they often stayed in the summer. He bought Ina a bicycle, so that she could explore the countryside and visit her parents at Glanton, and he took her with him to Oban for a holiday, and later to Norway and the Canaries. It was during this last trip that she visited Marion in Las Palmas.

Conrad kept his promise and Elizabeth inherited his money, but William did not live long to enjoy this change in the family fortunes.

Glanton House was very quiet and empty now. For thirty years it had echoed with the sound of young voices. Now all had gone out into the world, and William and Elizabeth were alone.

Chapter XI

SHIP'S SURGEON

'My road leads me seawards'
John Masefield: Roadways

(i)

When Will had finished his term as House Physician at Charing Cross Hospital, he began to look for an opening in general practice. While he was looking round he met a doctor friend who was interested in mental illness. This doctor had a patient whom he suspected of suffering from a mental disorder, and on whom he wished to keep a constant watch. He suggested to Will that he and the patient should both stay with him, ostensibly as guests, and that Will should keep an eye on the patient while the doctor was out. As Will had no appointment in view, he accepted the offer. The doctor had a pleasant house in the country, and the patient turned out to be a charming person, a retired army officer. Will found him a delightful companion, and at first enjoyed what appeared to be a sinecure. The officer seemed to be completely normal; he was an intelligent man, and he and Will had many interests in common. It was summer time, and they sat in the garden and went for walks, enjoying each other's company. This was all very well for a short time; it was a welcome holiday for Will. But after a week or two he became restive, and felt he was wasting his time, so he told the doctor he wished to leave. The doctor asked him to stay a little longer, and reluctantly Will agreed. A few days later he and the officer were sitting in the garden enjoying a chat when suddenly the patient jumped to his feet and announced in a stentorian voice, "I am Queen Elizabeth!" Will's vigil was not wasted after all.

In March 1896, he went to New York and back as ship's surgeon, and was paid £10 for the round voyage. He sailed from London in the <u>Manitoba</u>, 'a very large ship with saloon passengers only, and only eight of them.' On the return journey, however, there were sixty to seventy passengers. 'He fell in with some very nice people,' Elizabeth reported to Clara. Little did they then know what this meant. In the middle of May Will told his parents that he had become engaged to one of the passengers. The news did not please them. Will had known the girl for a very short time, and they felt he had been far too precipitate. They seem, too, to have had a premonition that she was not the right wife for him. 'He seems, poor fellow! to have been smitten at first sight, and perhaps was all the more hasty, as she is to return in a few weeks to Canada... Of course Will thinks her perfect.' Very soon after his return from New York Will joined the Union Line and sailed for South Africa in the <u>Greek</u>, but he asked his mother to invite his fiancée to Glanton, and this she did. The visit was not a success. A letter from Elizabeth to Clara reveals her intense disappointment and anxiety:

Will in Ship's Surgeon uniform

'I am sorry she did not turn out "all our fancy painted her". I certainly had made up my mind that she <u>must</u> be very <u>nice</u>, to please Will, both in appearance and every other way, and must own it was a severe disappointment when I saw her step from the conveyance –such a shabby little body – not in dress, that was neat enough excepting the <u>hat</u>, which was a "Dr. Jim" with a narrow band round it... I was so sorry for Papa. He went to the Station to meet her, and was quite prepared to receive her into his heart at once, but looked, to say the least, disappointed in the extreme when he saw her. I cannot see what there is about her to have taken Will's fancy so. She is not accomplished, neither plays nor sings, but from her own tale, it is evident she had taken possession of him at once, and been determined not to let him slip... Then although there was nothing <u>vulgar</u> in her manner here, it was <u>too free</u>. She was not an hour in the house till she was running upstairs <u>singing</u> and quite at home, and before she had got her things out of her bag said to me - "Now I want you to show me all over your house." Fancy! Certainly no shyness there. However, I told her I would not do that, it was not convenient.

Altogether I scarcely know what my verdict is. In many ways she is a sensible woman, but certainly not a sensitive one, and although she might have done as an acquaintance is not what I could wish in a relation. However, we did out best to entertain her, and be kind to her, <u>for Will's sake</u>... I feel a difficulty in writing to him, for I cannot tell a lie and say I can love her, besides there is time yet.'

Poor Elizabeth! Nowadays the young lady's interest in her fiancé's home would seem quite natural, and her lack of shyness and of drawing-room accomplishments would not be held against her, but she was too 'modern' for Elizabeth's taste. However, absence in this case did not make the heart grow fonder, and in March of the following year Will's parents heard, with great relief, that the engagement had been broken off 'by mutual consent.'

Will had intended to make only two or three voyages, but he loved the sea and continued as ship's surgeon for three years. His aunt Eliza had news of him through an acquaintance who had been a passenger in the <u>Greek</u>:

'He seems to enjoy the life. I heard his Praises sounded by the Newbigins. Mrs. Lill, their Aunt, had come home in the <u>Greek</u> and had made herself known to Willie. She says he is so kind to his Patients, he will sit up half the night with them and he saved a Lady from throwing herself out of the Cabin Window into the sea – her heart had been affected.'

In those days the Union Liners carried a cow, whose milk was reserved for invalids and children on the recommendation of the medical officer. The remaining passengers and the ship's company had only tinned sweetened milk, which Will disliked so much that for the rest of his life he took his tea without milk. On one of his voyages there was an outbreak of smallpox in the steerage, and Will had eleven cases under is care. He was never squeamish, and his years of medical training had hardened him to the unpleasant aspects of illness, but he confessed later that it took all his courage and determination to attend the worst affected patients. The stench and the sight of bodies so covered with suppurating sores that hardly an inch of clean skin was visible were enough to turn even Will's stomach. Of the eleven patients, only two died, and they had never been vaccinated. Those who had been vaccinated in infancy had the disease mildly, and no one who had been inoculated more recently caught it at all.

So much did Will enjoy this maritime existence that he might have been content to spend the rest of his life at sea, but the fates, in the shape of a theatrical company, decreed otherwise.

(ii)

In 1895, Mr W. J. Holloway, an actor-manager, took his company to South Africa. With him were his wife, his two daughters, Theodora and Juliet, who were members of the company, and his sixteen-year-old son John, who acted as treasurer and handyman. They were to play some of the then popular dramas such as The Bells, Quo Vadis and The Prisoner Of Zenda, but they were also including Shakespeare in their repertoire. Mr Holloway had long been a Shakespearean actor. He had played at the Lyceum with Sir Henry Irving, and on one occasion, when Irving was suddenly taken ill, was called upon to play the part of King Lear at a few hours' notice. He had been playing the Earl of Kent, but had not understudied Irving, so he was told that, as he could not be expected to become word-perfect in so short a time, he could read the part. But Mr. Holloway could not read without his glasses, and one could hardly put a pair of spectacles on the nose of an ancient British King! By an amazing feat of concentration and memory he made himself word-perfect and played the part with great success.

When he announced that he was going to produce Shakespeare in Johannesburg, pessimists in England shook their heads. The Transvaal, a Boer republic, was still new and undeveloped. Johannesburg less than ten years old, was a strange straggling conglomeration of tin shanties and new stone buildings, with no proper roads and no sanitation, and inhabited mostly by the rough characters involved in the gold rush. These people would not be interested in Othello or King Lear, and the tour would flop. So said the Jeremiahs, but they were wrong. For several weeks the company played to packed houses, and it seemed that the tour would be an outstanding success. That the success did not continue was due not to Shakespeare but to external events. Tension between the Boers and the 'uitlanders' was increasing every day, and when, in December 1895, it culminated in the catastrophic Jameson Raid, the company found themselves playing to half-empty houses. Boer guns were trained on the town, hordes of disorderly Kaffirs roamed the streets, and all sensible people kept to the shelter of their homes. So great was the danger that Mr. Holloway gave his son a revolver – not for self-defence, but to shoot his mother and sisters rather than let them fall into the hands of the Kaffirs. To add to the troubles there was a water famine; and a train-load of dynamite exploded just outside the town, killing several hundred people and rendering thousands homeless.

After five gruelling months in Johannesburg, the company moved on to Cape Town, and here, in the peaceful atmosphere of British territory, they again played to crowded houses and recouped the losses of their ill-fated Transvaal season.

In 1898, W. J. Holloway again took his company to South Africa. At the end of the tour they left Cape Town in the <u>Greek</u>, and during the voyage Dora hurt her arm and consulted the ship's medical officer – Dr Will Robertson. The injury was not serious, but the doctor said that he would like to see his patient again the following day – and the next day – and the next. It was amazing how many visits to the surgery that minor accident entailed. Will and Dora had fallen in love.

When the voyage came to an end they wrote to each other frequently and, by a stroke of luck, on a subsequent journey the company again travelled in the same ship as Will (the <u>Briton</u> this time) as far as Cape Town. They were going on to East London in the <u>Greek</u>, but Will had to return to England in the <u>Briton</u>. He came to the docks to see them off, and stayed on board until the last possible moment, even after all visitors had been ordered ashore. Then, taking his courage in both hands, he asked Dora to marry him, she accepted, and, without time even to kiss his betrothed, Will scrambled ashore just as the gangplank was about to be raised.

Dora wrote to him from East London, where they were unable to land for twenty-four hours on account of the rough seas:

> *I have been sitting in my deck chair all day reading and thinking of somebody – you may guess who – can you? I told Mother and*

Dad last night. They are very pleased. You know they like you very much.'

Dora was not yet quite used to being engaged; she began her letter formally, ' Dear Dr. Robertson.'

Will arrived in England at the end of August 1898 and spent his short leave at Glanton. While there, he suggested that his parents should meet him at Southampton at the end of his next trip and see his ship. Ina thought this an excellent idea, 'but the bother is that Mother has not got a nice winter mantle, she couldn't go in that dreadful thing she now has and it will be too late in the year (November) for her summer cape.' She wondered if the family could join together to buy a mantle as an advance Christmas present. Elizabeth was keen to go to Southampton, but William would not commit himself. It was some weeks before Ina was able to write to Clara:

> *'Papa has quite made up his mind to go south and is really quite excited about it. We never mentioned it to him until he began himself to speak of it for we feared he might be "contrary".'*

Once the master of the house had given his consent to the expedition, Elizabeth set about preparing her wardrobe. It seems that the family did buy the mantle for her:

> *'My mantle came yesterday,'* she wrote to Clara at the beginning of November. *'It is very nice... it is canvas cloth with a bright broche* pattern and some fur on it. I am making the skirt of a dress Emily gave me. It is one of Noble's 7/6 costume cloths... I enclose a bit of my dress – it looks very nice indeed. I have used the embossed velvet you wore at school to trim it – it just matches. I have not got my bonnet made yet. I have been making 3 night shirts for Papa – two are Flannelette. I have made them to reach his feet, so they ought to be comfortable.'*

Towards the end of November William and Elizabeth set out on their journey. They spent the first few days in London, Elizabeth staying with her friend, Mrs Barber, and William for some reason spending

---

*   *A pinstripe woven in the warp direction of the fabric used in cloth manufacture*

the first two nights at a temperance hotel near King's Cross before rejoining Elizabeth at Mrs Barber's house. It was while they were in London that they first met their future daughter-in-law. They faced the meeting with some misgivings. The news of Will's engagement to Dora had been received with mixed feelings at Glanton House. His parents were glad to know that he was likely at last to have a settled home life (he was now in his late thirties), but they had not forgotten his earlier unfortunate engagement. And now he had chosen an <u>actress</u>! They were not opposed to the theatre and though William and Elizabeth had probably seldom been inside one, living as they did so far from a city, the younger generation were ardent theatre-goers. But there still lingered in the minds of the old people, at least, a feeling that the morals of stage folk were inclined to be lax. What would she be like, this girl who had been born and bred in the world of the theatre? Could she possibly be the right wife for a respectable general practitioner?

Will and Dora met William at King's Cross, and great was his parents' relief when they were introduced to an attractive, unaffected and rather shy girl – very different from their preconceived idea of an actress. Dora was, in fact, a little scared of meeting her future parents-in-law.

> *'She seems very nice,'* William wrote to Clara, *'rather nice looking... Next day Will arranged for her to come and meet us and we took a walk to St. James's Park... She seems quiet and very pleasant.'*

Will returned to his ship, and a few days later William and Elizabeth followed.

> *'We went down to Southampton,'* wrote William, *'a glorious ride through Surrey and Hampshire and lovely scenery, the foliage being still on and the colours beautiful beyond description. We soon met with Will and set off after luncheon to view the grand ship "Briton." We saw all over the ship, down to the machinery also. She is certainly a huge and splendid vessel, the fittings very fine.'*

Soon after their visit Will sailed again to South Africa on what was to be his last voyage, while Dora remained in her father's company.

Will was not yet in a position to support a wife, and he realised that, with marriage in view, he must give up the sea and find a practice in England. After several short periods as assistant or locum he went, in March 1899, to Selston, a colliery village in Nottinghamshire, where he lodged in a farmhouse. He did not care for his surroundings, and felt rather lonely, but a month later Elizabeth reported that he seemed more content. 'He is getting a few cases and expects to get a Club very soon, which will bring him about £40 or £50 year.' In April, Dora, with her sister as chaperone, spent a few days in nearby Pinxton, so that the engaged couple could have a little time together before the company returned to South Africa. (They sailed on Friday 13th May which the superstitious members of the theatrical profession regarded as an ill omen, but the tour proved very successful financially, though certainly not lacking in adventures).

It was perhaps partly to cheer Will up after Dora's departure that his father paid him a short visit at Whitsun. He had a very unpleasant journey.

> 'I had a terrible business to reach my destination,' he wrote to Emily, 'losing my road and feeling dreadfully exhausted... I did not reach Will's abode till about 10 p.m., and, poor fellow, he had been to Nottingham to meet me, but that horrid excursion train was so late that he left (and this was a journey of nearly an hour by rail), then he went down to Pinxton and also wired, and did I know not what all to make matters right for me. Then at the last he had just (after his 2nd or 3rd run down to Pinxton) left the station about 5 or 10 minutes before my train arrived there... I almost gave up the ghost before I reached Will's lodgings, having my bag to carry and up hill and off the right road and in the dark, but (as matters always might be worse) without rain overhead.'

Poor William! He was, after all, 78, and unused to railway travel, and he was suffering from a cold and sore throat.

He did not think much of Selston, and did not stay there long. The weather was miserable, his throat was troubling him, and he was fretting about some of his patients in Glanton.

> *'It is a wretched looking village,'* he wrote after his return, *'and the surroundings not attractive, but Will does not seem to mind that very much, if only he could get practice, which I am glad to say he seems likely to get gradually... I felt sorry to have to leave dear Will so soon and I felt also as if I had been ungrateful for so much kindness as both Clara and he between them nearly paid all my expenses. I cannot describe the village or give you any idea of Will's situation. The neighbourhood is surrounded by collieries, which however do not disfigure the country as they do in Northumberland and Durham. Still the chief inhabitants are colliers and "Club" practice is the order of the day thereabouts. Fees consequently small, nor will there be any opening for Will to obtain one of these "Clubs" at present.'*

Will did not like Selston either, though he had tried to hide the fact from his father. In May 1899, a notice had appeared in an Australian newspaper (Dora had been born in Melbourne) announcing that

> *'on her return from the South African tour for which she is now preparing Miss Theodora Holloway, eldest daughter of Mr. W.J. Holloway, will be married to Dr. Robertson, who intends to settle in the Midlands. Dr. Robertson was the medical officer on the steamer by which the company recently travelled.'*

But Will did not settle in the Midlands. Apart from his dislike of Selston, he did not feel that he could ever build up a successful practice there, so he began to look around for something better and eventually became assistant to a doctor in Clapham, in South London.

Chapter XII
WAR AND OTHER ADVENTURES

'Days of danger, nights of waking'
Scott: The Lady of the Lake

Meanwhile, there was more trouble in South Africa, and when Mr. Holloway produced <u>Othello</u> in Johannesburg the audience hissed at the playing of the British national anthem. By June 1899, war with the Boers seemed inevitable, but Dora, writing to Will from Port Elizabeth, still hoped that it might be averted:

> *'There are all sorts of rumours coming from Johannesburg. First it's "war", then "no war", but one cannot tell what will happen. I should say Kruger will hardly be so foolish as to enter into war with England. If it does come, how terrible it will be. All the English first sent are sure to be killed, tho' of course in the end Kruger would be beaten, but do not, dearest, be anxious about me, as Dad had arranged not to go further than Kimberley if there is trouble.'*

Social life in Port Elizabeth continued as usual, and Dora was becoming weary of the never-ending entertainment provided for the company:

> *'Mother and I went to the ball the other night. We stayed only a short time, but I felt just worn out the next day. We are invited to another next Friday, but only Julie is going, as we shall be playing As You Like It and Rosalind is about as much as I can manage in one evening.'*

Dora, under her professional name of Cecil Arden, scored an outstanding success as Rosalind.

When war came, Will applied for the post of medical Officer to the Military Department, and Sir Henry Waterhouse, one of the surgeons under whom he had worked at Charing Cross, wrote his testimonial:

> *'Mr. Robertson was one of out most distinguished students at Charing Cross Hospital, was Prizeman in several classes, and*

91

held with credit the post of Resident House Physician. I know of no young medical man whom, from intimate personal knowledge, I could more cordially recommend for such a post… He is quite a first class man.'

Will did not, however, obtain the post.

In England, not everyone approved of the war. William wrote to Emily on Boxing Day 1899:

'This dreadful war is the great topic. Dare I say I sympathise with the poor Boers quite as much as with our own troops. This is of course high treason in the opinion of many, but I am thankful to say not of everyone. Neither side is faultless.'

Dora and her parents were still in Africa when war broke out, but it had little effect on the theatrical business and they continued to play to crowded houses. They were, however, subjected to adventures unconnected with the war. In October 1899 they left East London in a gale, and Dora and Juliet were terribly seasick when they were taken out to the <u>Norman</u> in a tug. When they arrived at Port Elizabeth they were not allowed ashore as there was plague at Delagoa Bay, where they had called, and they had a suspected case on board, so their ship was put into quarantine. This proved to be a false alarm – the suspected case was suffering from measles – and they were soon out of quarantine, but still they could not land on account of the rough seas.

It was while they were staying at Deal's Hotel in East London that they suffered their first nerve-racking experience, which Dora described in a letter to Will:

'I woke very suddenly, wide awake at once, and my first thought was that the hotel was on fire. It was just as if someone had told me, I was so positive about it, and then when I rushed to the window and saw the smoke and flames I felt almost paralysed with terror… our window was right over the fire. Poor Julie was in a terrible state of fear. After calling Jack, I told Julie to take on half of the hotel while I took the other, and in a very few minutes we had everyone awake. They say that if I had been too

frightened to think what to do, or had waited to get some clothes on before rousing the proprietor, the hotel must have been burnt. As it was they were just in time to keep the fire from spreading to the main building... You can imagine how very surprised I was on Monday when Mr. Deal presented me with a beautiful diamond and pearl brooch. With it was a card on which was written, "Many thanks to Miss Holloway for saving my hotel from destruction by her timely alarm." I am not a little proud of that, tho' I don't think I really deserved it... At the same time Mr. Deal gave Julie a sweet little gold bracelet "for kind assistance" – and she certainly did scream, poor child, but strangely enough she seems to have recovered from the shock sooner that I do... How much I want to be with you, to be looked after and taken care of. I have had too much excitement. I want to be quiet and rest.'

But it was not long before Dora was involved in another terrifying experience. They were travelling to Kimberley by train when:

'between 11 and 12 o'clock this morning Julie, Miss Estcourt and I were sitting in our compartment busied with printing photographs, when suddenly the train lurched violently to one side, then to the other, then we felt a collision, and after about a minute more came to a standstill. Our coach, all ladies in it except Dad and Jack, had come off the rails. The underneath part, wheels, springs, etc., are all smashed to pieces, and just outside our cabin the carriage itself is all broken in. Our coach was in the middle of the train, and the engine driver did not stop till Mr. Meillie of our company rang the alarm on the next coach, and we were dragged along 400 yards off the rails over two little viaducts and a bridge. The rail just here is built high up and it is simply wonderful how we did not go right over the embankment. Coming round one sharp curve we were only saved by a water tank, for the engine which we collided with, smashing both the tank and the carriage, then the iron bridge, is not only injured but the stone coping at the side is all knocked down. We cannot think how we ever crossed the viaducts. They are simply rails supported on iron stanchions with wooden sleepers going from side to side. The wheels on one side of the carriage have cut through the sleeper in the middle and of course the other wheels were simply

on nothing. The guard says had we gone on another fifty yards nothing could have saved us... It was an awful five minutes and I was quite certain our last on earth. It is now nearly six o'clock. They sent the engine for men and have been all this time raising the coach and removing the debris. All the wheels and under-workings of the coach were removed, such as was left of them, the rest being scattered round the desert, then the coach was raised on trollies, and they have got it a few yards down the line, and it is now broken down again so when we shall get on is very doubtful. Food is running very short, some people are without any. We still have some bread and some wine. Fortunately there was a coach with only one gentleman in so we had to pack up all our things and go into that.

Later...
It is now about nine o'clock and we are off once more... The guard has told us that ten yards further on nothing could have saved us from going over the embankment. We are all feeling very much shaken now it is all over, but the ladies all behaved splendidly... I did not feel frightened at all, though I felt sure it was all over with us. We three girls just sat quietly. I made them put their feet up on the seats, for hearing the crash into the water tank I thought it was a collision, and I always heard so many people had their legs crushed and broken by the seats being jammed together in railway accidents, and Julie immediately let the windows down, so that the glass should not break in our faces.'

Dora's reaction to these two hair-raising experiences was typical of her. She was always a nervous woman, yet in a real emergency she never failed to remain calm and rise to the occasion.

Even the railway accident was not the last of the ordeals the company experienced in South Africa. They were caught in Kimberley when it was besieged in 1899, and the town was only a few miles from the Orange Free State, which was Boer territory. They could not venture into the streets during the day, and from their hotel windows watched truckloads of dead, British and Boer, being driven through town.

Many years later Dora described her South African adventures to the three young sons of her husband's cousin. They listened, enthralled and starry-eyed, then one of them said, 'Oh, Cousin Dora, what a <u>lovely</u> life you've had!'

Mr. Holloway and his company managed to extricate themselves from the beleaguered town, and were back in England by December 1899. They were playing at Oxford in May 1900 on the night when news was received of the relief of Mafeking, and the ladies of the company needed a strong male escort to see them safely through the streets crowded with hysterical, shouting, flag-waving students. The whole country was in a state of wild excitement. William wrote to Emily:

> *'London certainly has gone mad over Mafeking, and yet no blame to it. The provinces have been just as wild. Poor Mrs. B.P.[Baden Powell] must be tired of the demonstrations at her abode, but I dare say will put up with it till the people tire also... Oh! that this sickening and woeful war were at an end. I agree with you about what ought to be the settlement of affairs but our Government and the country are demented.'*

Early in 1900 Will took Dora to Glanton. Though she had met her fiancé's parents and two of his sisters – Emily and Florence – in London, their contact had been brief. Now she had to face the far greater ordeal of spending a few days in the Robertsons' own home, where she would be under the close scrutiny, not only of William and Elizabeth, but also of three as yet unknown sisters-in-law-to-be. She later confessed that she felt very scared as the wagonette approached Glanton House, and her apprehensiveness was not lessened when, with her first words, she made a slight <u>gaffe</u>. It was a cold, blustery day, and Elizabeth, kissing her future daughter-in-law, said, 'Come in, my dear. You must be starved' – using the word in its old sense of 'cold'. Dora, ignorant of the north country idiom, replied, 'Oh no, thank you, we had a good meal on the train.' Elizabeth, however, with her usual tact and charm, soon put the nervous blushing girl at her ease, and the visit passed very happily.

About a month later, in February, William had a nasty accident. There had been severe storms and blizzards (how often we hear of the severity of the winter weather at Glanton!) and William slipped on the frozen snow outside the back door, dislocating his shoulder and breaking a rib.

95

Dr Watson, from Whittingham, was summoned, and tried to reduce the dislocation without an anaesthetic, Elizabeth being unwilling, for some reason, to let William have chloroform. But 'he could not stand the pain and at last it was given, and the joint yielded immediately and father bore the chloroform splendidly.' Ina came from Newcastle for a few days to help her mother, and Elizabeth also found a girl to help in the house. 'She is most useful,' Elizabeth wrote to Emily. 'She is slow but very willing and quiet.' They also found a lad to look after the pony and stable.

The storm was one of the worst Elizabeth remembered. She could not get out of the back door until John Younger, who lived nearby, cut a way through. 'This has been a terrible storm,' she wrote. 'Mr. McIntosh was worse – the wreathe [snow drift] was above his front door.' It reminded her of a storm a quarter of a century earlier when William was caught in a blizzard at the Pyke, a mile away, and could not get home until the next day.

William was in his eightieth year, and it took him some time to recover from his injuries. In the meantime Dr Watson attended his patients. On 29th March he wrote to Emily:

> 'My shoulder is far from right yet, if it ever will be, but my rib is all right and I am riding about, with a little help at mounting.'

His disability was not improved by the weather, which continued to be appalling:

> 'Here we are still in the midst of Winter, snow all over, and at this moment it is actually snowing... the frost is still keen. When is this dreadful weather to come to an end.'

CHAPTER XIII

THE END OF AN ERA

'But, O the heavy change now thou art gone'
John Milton: L'Allegro

(i)

When war broke out, Jack was sent to South Africa with his detachment of the Mounties, and arrived in Cape Town in March 1900.

> *'I sadly fear,'* wrote William to Emily, *'he will have some warm work before this bloody strife is ended. Oh! may he be preserved in the midst of danger from all ill, from sickness, wounds and death, and be restored to us to receive the warmest of welcomes. I live in constant dread, I confess, but may it please God that our beloved Boy may escape injury.'*

Two months later he wrote:

> *'I expect he has been engaged in scenes of stern conflict with the foe since his last letter was despatched from Springfontein. Evidently his corps has been in the thick of the fight with Hamilton [General Sir Bruce Hamilton] . I earnestly hope and pray that he has been preserved from danger both in fire and in the midst of sickness and privation.'*

Sickness, indeed, was a greater risk than battle, for thousands of British soldiers had fallen victim to typhoid, and more died of this disease than of wounds.

While in South Africa, Jack sent home to his parents a cutting from a Port Elizabeth newspaper reviewing W. J. Holloway's production of <u>Hamlet</u>, knowing that they would be interested in the success of Dora's family.

> *'Lovers of Shakespearian plays were afforded "something rich and rare" on Thursday and last evening when the local stage*

was graced by the finest performance of Shakespeare's immortal tragedy "Hamlet" it has been the privilege of Port Elizabethans to witness here... Mr. Holloway's rendering was full of nobility and meaning. Every word, every gesture was hung upon with intense interest. One admires and learns, but cannot criticise... Mr. Holloway's rendering of Hamlet may be described as great... The "Ophelia" of Miss Juliet Sydney [Dora's sister] was a beautiful pourtrayal, and characteristic of this gifted young actress. In the scene of madness she excelled... it was all gentleness, sweetness and infinite pathos.'

Jack came safely through the war, and for some reason was demobilised in January 1901, though the war continued until the following year. In Glanton he was regarded as a conquering hero, and was given a reception in the village hall. He was home just in time to be best man at Will's wedding.

```
From.                                      Jan. 19th. 1901.

        Newcastle Daily Journal.

           HOME-COMING OF A VOLUNTEER

                Rejoicings at Glanton.


        The usually quiet village of Glanton was quite en fete on
Thursday, when Mr. John Robertson, son of Dr. Robertson, of Glanton,
arrived home from South Africa, where he has been serving in the
war. He had been on the Mounted Police in Canada for fourteen years,
and was one of the first to volunteer for active service, and joined
the Canadian Mounted Rifles. Mr. Robertson has been repeatedly in
action and has had a horse shot under him, several of his comrades
also being shot by his side.

        As the venerable doctor and his family are held in great re-
spect by Glantonians, they were determined to give the gallant sol-
dier a hearty welcome. The village was quite gay with bunting, flags,
etc. On arriving at the station a carriage and pair were in waiting
to convey him by way of the Dean and Well House Road. He was met at
the outskirts of the village by a large crowd, who gave him a hearty
reception, the horses being unyoked and the carriage dragged through
the village to the doctor's residence. The Rev. R.H.Davidson was pres-
ent to receive him, and on behalf of the inhabitants of Glanton gave
Mr. Robertson a cordial welcome.

        Mr. Robertson thanked them for the warm reception they had
given him, which, he said, was quite unlooked for.
```

Will and Dora were married at the church on Turnham Green on 31st January 1901. This happy event was somewhat marred by extraneous circumstances. Queen Victoria had died a few days earlier, and London was plunged in mourning, but the wedding could not be postponed because Dora's parents were about to sail for South Africa. To add to the prevailing gloom, the English climate had been doing its worst, and there had been heavy snow. Fortunately on the wedding-day there was a temporary improvement though it was still bitterly cold. Florence who attended the wedding with Elizabeth and Emily, sent Clara an account of it:

'I know you are all excitement to hear about the wedding... To begin with we all have a beautiful frosty dry day and so got to the Church with clean shoes and petticoats, and hair reasonably in curl. Everything passed off very quietly and pleasantly, there being no one in the Church except the few friends invited... Dora looked very nice indeed. She wore a long fawn or beaver coloured coat, which was lined with pale blue silk. Her dress was of the same coloured silk poplin with a crêpe de chine bodice of blue and a bolero the same colour and material as the skirt. Her hat matched her dress and was trimmed with velvet and ostrich feathers. There were no bridesmaids... Juliet had a crushed strawberry frieze dress with white silk revers and vest, a hat to match of velvet and a white ostrich feather in it and a grey cape. She looked very pretty, I thought. She is a very jolly girl. I like the family more the better I know them. Mrs. H. wore a black net dress, violet velvet hat and ermine cape. The other guests were very plainly attired and we did not feel out of it at all. Mother looked very nice and so did Em in her new blue gown... Will looks so happy, it has been quite a pleasure to see him... Everyone is in mourning for the poor old Queen and the place looks most mournful, it gives one the hump. At the present moment there is a cornet and fiddle in the court outside playing the Dead March. Somehow her death came as a shock to everyone tho' at her age it might have been expected... It will take a while to get accustomed to think and speak of a King.'

Will's partner was an awkward character, and would only allow him one day off for the wedding, so there would be no honeymoon. Dora said good-bye to her parents and her brother and sister, knowing that she would not see them again for many months, and accompanied her bridegroom to a tall, gaunt, cold house in Gauden Road, Clapham, in a neighbourhood where she did not know a soul. It was an unromantic beginning to marriage.

They lived in Gauden Road until 1908, when Will bought a house in Bedford Road, half a mile away and set up practice on his own. In later years his former partner's practice was taken over by a young Welsh doctor who became Will's life-long friend.

(ii)

The year 1901, which had begun so happily with the marriage of Will and Dora and Jack's safe return from war, was to bring great sorrow to Glanton House. William had not been really well since his accident in 1900, and early in the following year he became very ill with bronchitis. By April he was obviously a dying man. Clara and Jack were at home, Conrad White let Ina go to Glanton to help, and Will somehow persuaded his partner to give him a few days off. Elizabeth wrote to Emily in London:

> 'Father has just fallen asleep after partaking of a nice little bowl of soup... This had been a most anxious and terrible week to us all, for dear Father has been very near the Borderland and the prospect of parting was very bitter. It has pleased God to spare him for a little while, but I cannot close my eyes to the fact that at most it cannot be long... Father is certainly in the meantime much better – the heart symptoms remarkably relieved and the Bronchitis yielding, but the cough is still troublesome... his appetite, too, is improving... Tim [Clara] will have told you all our arrangements. She has been a great comfort to me, and Ina too, poor girls. And oh the relief to have Jack home and to have dear Will! It was good of Will to come so promptly and stay. I am sure it did much to bring Father so far forward as he is today.'

By the middle of May it was clear that William could not live long, and Will again went to Glanton and stayed until after the funeral, helping with the disposal of his father's drugs and instruments. Dora did not

100

accompany him, and on 27th May wrote:

'When first I saw what a bright and beautiful day it was, I felt it was out of place with the sadness you must all be feeling, but now, dear, it has come to me that the glory of the sun and sky, the song of the birds, seem like a message of promise from Heaven, telling of the beautiful world to which your dear father is gone and of the happiness that is his now.'

William Robertson's tombstone in Bolton Church yard

'I summon up remembrance of things past'
Shakespeare: Sonnets

CHAPTER I

FIRST IMPRESSIONS

'The younger generation will come knocking at my door'
Ibsen: The Master-Builder

In the early hours of 17th May 1904, a baby was born in Clapham. The infant weighted 10 ¼ pounds and had lungs of proportionate size. It yelled incessantly day and night, and Will and Dora wondered why they had ever thought it would be nice to have a baby in the house. I was the baby.

Elizabeth was in London at this time, and on 21st May she made the acquaintance of her first grandchild.

> *'I went to Clapham to see the new importation... Well! It is a baby!... It might be five or six weeks old. Its clothes will not fit it long... Nurse says it is the largest child she had ever had.'*

In view of my screaming propensities, it was hardly surprising that I was not taken to Glanton that summer. My first visit took place the following year, by which time I had apparently become less vocal, though no less hefty; I weighed one and a half stone. My only surviving great-aunt, Eliza, now in her eighties, came from Alnwick to see her great-niece and was a little disconcerted by the size of the pudding-like object that waddled across the floor to inspect her. It would not have been quite nice to describe the child as 'fat' – an unladylike word – so she said, euphemistically, *'Isn't the baby stout?'* She died later the same year, so did not live to know that her great-niece, having once lost her baby fat, would grow thinner and thinner until by the time she was grown up she was, like most Robertsons, 'lean and lang and lanky.'

That was in 1905. From then until 1963 there was only one year in which I did not visit Glanton, and before I went to school I was often left there for two or three months. It became, for me, a second and much loved home and 'Going to Glanton' was the highlight of my year.

Dora and Joyce in the Glanton garden

It was a long and tedious journey by train. My parents always arrived early at King's Cross to be sure of finding an empty compartment, and, when I was a baby, held me up at the window in the hope that other passengers would be deterred from entering a compartment where they would have to endure the long journey to Newcastle in the company of a lusty infant. It generally worked. At Newcastle we changed to another train which took us as far as Alnmouth. Here we had to change again for Alnwick, a journey of only about seven minutes, then out we all bundled again and piled into the local train to Glanton. To me this was the most exciting part of the journey. Near Edlingham the train slowed down and our guard leaned out of his van and handed a pole to another railwayman standing beside the track who gave him what appeared to be an identical pole in exchange. I did not know – nor do I now – what was the object of this operation but it never lost its fascination. Then there was the long tunnel, when we hastily shut the window before the carriage filled with smoke, and the engine gave an ear-splitting shriek which continued until we emerged into daylight.

When at last we reached Glanton station our old friend Carr, the porter, was there to greet us. The bulk of our luggage – a huge trunk – had been sent in advance by goods train, but even so there would be several suitcases, a picnic basket, Dora's dressing-case (an incredibly heavy contraption of purple leather fitted with innumerable little silver-topped glass jars), two bicycles, my father's cameras – never less than two – his boxes of plates, a tripod and other photographic equipment, not to mention the child and numerous toys which had been brought to keep her quiet during the long journey. One did not 'travel light' in those days. Why should one? There were always rows of porters vying for the privilege of carrying one's luggage in exchange for a twopenny tip. All our paraphernalia were somehow piled into the wagonette that had been sent to meet us. This belonged to Foggin, the village saddler, and we drove up to Glanton House enveloped in an unforgettable odour of leather and horse which seemed to emanate from the wagonette, from Foggin himself and, one assumes, from the horse. It was an exciting smell, quite different from the smell of London's horse-drawn traffic, and associated forever in a child's mind with the fact that we had arrived. On the way up the hill to the village we would see women working in the fields, dressed in light blue smocks and large floppy hats, the traditional costume for women land-workers* in Northumberland in those days.

The 'low gate' – the main gate that led to the drive and the front of the house – would be open for us, and, as we clattered up to the front door, there would erupt from the house a vast multitude of people; Grannie, a bevy of aunts, perhaps an uncle or two. I suppose this impression of a seething mob of aunts and uncles must have been formed at a later date, for during my earliest years not many of them can have been at home. Alfred and Jack were in Canada, Conrad was in Birmingham, Marion in the Canaries and Florence in London. Nevertheless, our arrival at Glanton is indelibly associated in my mind with a surge of excited and rather overpowering elders. As the swarm of human bees buzzed round us, there followed an orgy of kissing. With so many kissers and three kissees, it was inevitable that some confusion should arise and it frequently happened that one found oneself embraced several times by the same aunt, while another, less pushing – Clara, probably – had not been kissed at all. When this osculatory ceremony was satisfactorily concluded we were escorted to the best bedroom, supplied with hot

---

*   *Bondagers*

105

water in a brass can, and left in comparative peace to remove the grime acquired during eight or nine hours of travel; only comparative peace, because every few minutes an aunt would look in to ask, 'Did you have a good journey?,' 'Are you very tired?' and 'How is little Joyce?' Their excitement, at the annual visit of their beloved eldest brother, was as great as mine. Then to the dining-room where the table was loaded with girdle scones, baps, heather honey, two or three kinds of jam, and cakes – all, of course, home-made. There would always be a roaring fire in the large black-leaded grate, even in the summer Northumbrian evenings can be chilly, and all the family were fire-worshippers – like Emily, who had missed her open fire in Germany.

My recollections of the earlier holidays are naturally hazy, but the house and its furnishings changed little during the next sixty years. The hall was narrow and rather dark, the crepuscular light being due partly to panes of multicoloured glass in the front door which, in my young days, I thought surpassingly beautiful. The dining-room – the general living room, for the drawing-room was used only on special occasions – was almost completely filled by a billiard table, which served as a dining table, nor was it too big when all the family were at home. In those early days it was covered with a crimson cloth edged with a fringe and bobbles, later to be replaced by a drugget*. A huge mahogany sideboard, backed by a mirror, took up one side of the room and on it were the inevitable mats, a large black clock (which did not work) and two German-Victorian bronze horsemen. On the mantelpiece were numerous knick-knacks sitting on a felt runner with a valance of beadwork, no doubt the result of many hours' labour on the part of Elizabeth or one of her daughters. The walls were largely concealed by oil-paintings in massive gilt frames. These had come from the home of Conrad White, who considered himself a connoisseur of art and had acquired a sizeable collection of paintings, most of which he had bequeathed to the Laing Art Gallery in Newcastle. Those at Glanton House were, one assumes, the 'leftovers'. The room boasted only two comfortable chairs (comfortable by Victorian standards, that is). One, which had been William's preserve, was so large that the only way to achieve any degree of comfort was to curl oneself up into a ball on its capacious leather seat. The other, like the proverbial dachshund, had its legs too near the ground, and was the height of discomfort. As, however, these chairs were nearly always occupied by the

---

*   *Coarse woven fabric used as a floor or table covering*

Drawing-room Glanton House

current cats and dogs, it was seldom that a mere human could make use of them. To inconvenience an animal at Glanton House was unthinkable; <u>we</u> must sit round the dining-table in hard upright chairs. But, as the only illumination was from an oil lamp hanging over the middle of the table there was, in any case, no alternative in the evening if one wished to read or pursue any other useful occupation. With a roaring fire, the shutters closed, and perhaps eight or nine people clustered round the table, the room would become unbearably hot. Surreptitiously we would edge away from the fire, and – just by accident, of course – leave the door open an inch or two. *'Are you warm enough, dear?'* a solicitous aunt would ask. *'There's an awful draught.'* And firmly the door would be closed.

If important, or little-known, visitors were expected, a fire would be lit in the drawing-room, where the fireplace was draped with heavy curtains of russet velvet. On the mantelpiece – also covered in velvet – were a number of china ornaments, and the lustres* with which the

---

*   *Lustres are elaborate candle holders produced in pairs to set on a mantle*

young children had played so happily in days gone by. Two glass-fronted cabinets housed more ornamental china, and every inch of flat surface was occupied by a family photograph, each on its little mat. There were two Chippendale chairs (carefully concealed under faded cretonne covers), several attractive, if uncomfortable, occasional chairs with seats of tapestry or beadwork, some small tables with fringed cloths, and, of course, an upright piano, without which no Victorian home was complete. Of the walls little was to be seen, for they were hidden behind a motley collection of photographs, watercolours and china plates in plush mounts. It was all hopelessly old-fashioned, highly uncomfortable – and quite charming.

On the walls of the wide staircase were more large oil-paintings and even the lavatory, halfway up the stairs, was decorated with pictures. At the foot of the staircase stood an enormous square iron stove which had, I suppose, been used for heating at some early date but which in my day was merely an ornament, if such a word could be applied to anything so cumbersome and ugly. It merely took up space in the narrow hall but it had always been there so there it must remain. Even when Clara fell downstairs and cut her head open on the ugly brute, it did not occur to anyone to remove it.

The guests' bedroom where my parents slept, and where I, no doubt, had a cot until I was considered old enough to share a bed with an aunt, was the brightest room in the house. It looked out over the garden to Whittingham Vale and the distant hills, and was the only room from which this lovely view was not hidden by trees. The huge brass bedstead had heavy tapestry side-curtains which in the daytime were tastefully draped across the pillows. When, at a more mature age, I visited Glanton House by myself, I was given the doubtful privilege of sleeping in this bed. 'It's a good feather bed,' an aunt assured me, 'and very comfortable.' Perhaps she had never tried it. Perhaps it had been a good feather bed once. My own impression was that I was lying on a slab of concrete, and as for the feather mattress – when I lay on it one feather went one way, one the other, and I was left on the concrete slab. It was quite the most uncomfortable bed I had ever had the misfortune to meet. But then I am not a Victorian, and perhaps (unlike the bed) I am soft.

As in all the rooms, the furniture was massive. When I was about two years old I cut my head open on the wardrobe door, and it was many years before the hair grew again on the scar. On the marble-topped wash-stand were a china jug and basin, and in my early days there was a faithful maid called Hannah (daughter of John Younger) who arrived at 7am and brought hot water in brass cans to each room at 8 o'clock. There <u>was</u> a bathroom, but a hot bath was a luxury in which one seldom indulged, for there was only one tap – the cold one. Hot water had to be carried up from the kitchen by the long-suffering Hannah in an outsize can known as 'the flagon,' and it took at least six flagonfuls to produce a barely adequate bath. Moreover, one could not have a morning bath because the kitchen range had only just been lit, and in the evening it had gone out, so the only possible bathing time was in the afternoon, after a large mid-day meal.

It was not until the 1940s that electricity was installed. Until then one relied on oil lamps downstairs and went to bed by candle-light. Even as a small child I liked to read in bed, and more than once I was hauled over the coals for keeping late hours; my burnt-down candle gave me away. Lamps and candle-sticks were of brass, like the water cans, and several times a week Hannah would be seen cleaning and polishing and trimming wicks. Cooking was done in the kitchen range or on an oil stove, and when, just before the Second World War, the range was replaced by a Rayburn, the aunts regretted the change. Nothing cooked so well as in the old kitchener, they complained. It was not until much later that they acquired an electric cooker, and even then they did most of the cooking on the oil stove. Porridge, they asserted, could not be cooked properly by electricity. Porridge must, of course, be the real thing, made with oatmeal and stirred with a wooden stick called a 'thivel'; no 'quick porage oats' for them. They ate it in the north country fashion, with cold milk in a cup into which one dipped a spoonful of porridge.

The aunts were all good, plain cooks, and took the culinary chores in turn, a week at a time. The aunt on duty would disappear into the nether regions after breakfast and not emerge until lunch was served. One did not go hungry at Glanton House. For breakfast there would be a large bowl of porridge, followed by bacon or sausage; for lunch, the main meal of the day, there would be roast meat or a stew, a suet pudding, a pastry jam roll, or something equally filling. Afternoon tea was a major meal of bread and jam, scones and cakes, and at 8 o'clock one sat down to a 'light' repast of eggs or cold meat, more bread and more scones. In the soft fruit season there would be strawberries or raspberries for supper, but at other times fresh fruit seldom appeared on the table. They were not fond of vegetables, apart from potatoes and peas, and, though they always cooked other vegetables (mostly of the root variety) for their guests, there were barely enough to go round. It was not a case of cheese-paring – they were the most generous of folk, and they had a large garden where vegetables of all kinds were going to seed – but they judged their guests' tastes by their own. The meals they provided, so full of starch, so lacking in vitamin C, would no doubt horrify students of nutrition in this diet-conscious age, yet they had been brought up on this fare all their lives, and most of them lived in perfect health to a ripe old age – nor did they ever grow fat!

CHAPTER II

A PRIDE OF AUNTS

'Tisn't beauty, so to speak.. Some women'll stay in a man's memory if
they once walked down a street'
Kipling: Traffics and Discoveries

The aunt I knew best when I was a child was Florence, because she was living in London. By this time she had her own flat in Highbury, where I sometimes spent a week-end, and she came to dinner with us about once a month. On one occasion she came on my birthday, and my father had opened a bottle of Champagne to celebrate the event. After drinking my health, Florence put down her glass, screwed up her nose and said, 'It isn't <u>bad</u> – but I prefer ginger beer.' None of the aunts really appreciated alcohol, perhaps because they had never had it in their young days. William could not afford it, though he was not teetotal on principle. When he injured his shoulder, Emily sent him a small bottle of liqueur, which he greatly enjoyed and drank all himself because Elizabeth did not like it – or so she said. A few years ago I took my aunts a bottle of sherry, which appeared to give them great pleasure. 'We'll keep it for Sunday,' they said. The great day came, the cork was drawn, there was a last minute hunt for wine glasses. 'Isn't this a treat?' said Emily, as she handed me my sherry – in a liqueur glass. Ina threw back her head and downed hers in one go, as if it were Schnapps. No one was offered the other half (or should I say quarter?).

As a small child I was a little bit scared of Emily. She loved children and was, I am sure, very kind to her little niece, but she was impatient and quick-tempered and, to the shy, sensitive child I then was, seemed rather fierce. It was Emily who appeared in the garden one day when I was having a rather noisy game with some little friends and said, 'Don't shriek, child. Robertsons don't shriek.' She was proud of her clan. For perhaps the only time in my life I wished I were not a Robertson, and, young as I was, I could not help thinking she was being a little unfair. When she and her two eldest brothers were up to their pranks, there must have been plenty of shrieking in that garden, and certainly our Highland ancestors shrieked when they were raiding the neighbouring clans! Of course, Emily was not really fierce. She was, in fact, very soft-hearted, even sentimental.

Clara was known in the family as 'Tim.' As a very small child just beginning to talk, she heard someone mention Chillingham Castle and the name fascinated her. 'Timmy Tastle,' she repeated in her baby language. She liked the sound of this so much that for days she went round the house singing to herself 'Timmy Timmy Tastle' to the tune of 'Ring a ring o' roses', and for ever after her brothers and sisters called her Timmy or Tim. When I was beginning to talk I had a passion for the letter 'p' so Auntie Tim became Auntie Pim, and Auntie Pim she remained to me (and later to my cousin) for the rest of her life. She was a shy retiring woman, always sweet and gentle. Less adventurous than her sisters, she was one to be seen and not heard. Because of her diffidence she was less easy to get to know than her more extrovert sisters and it was not until I was grown up that I realised that, under her quiet, self-effacing manner, she was a woman of strong character. When differences arose among the sisters and tempers frayed, as happens in the most united of families, it was Clara, sitting forgotten as she placidly went on with her sewing, who put in the gentle word that brought the argument to an amicable conclusion.

After her uncle Conrad's death in 1905, Ina stayed at home for four years and was very popular with her small niece. She had a wonderful way with children. All the aunts played with me but the others played sedately. There was nothing sedate about Ina. Holding up her voluminous ankle-length skirts, she would race me to the bottom of the garden, or play hide-and-seek round the laurel bush in the middle of the lawn, laughing and – dare I say it – shrieking as much as her niece. In 1909

Ina

financial necessity obliged her to seek some employment and, as she too felt the wanderlust, she took a post as governess with an English family in Coimbatore in India. Here she revelled in the warmth and sunshine. In spite of having been brought up in the rigours of the Northumbrian climate – or perhaps because of it – all the family were sun-worshippers,

Young Hight with Ina

and their only complaint against their beloved Glanton was that it was seldom really warm.

Soon Ina was urgently in need of more summer clothes and asked Emily to send her 'a white linen or drill skirt, *40 inches long*.' English families in India kept up with the fashions current in England, and Ina noted that 'the sleeves of the ladies are now mostly diminished in size.' The full sleeves of the early Edwardian days were 'out.'

After six months Ina's job came to an end and she returned to England for a short time, but the following year she was off to India again with a family called Hight, who had a coffee and rubber plantation in the Shevaroy Hills. She became very fond of her pupil, and of all the family but, although she enjoyed the climate and the novelty of her surroundings, she never really settled down and her letters suggest that she was homesick and could not adapt herself to the way of life in India. 'Ina doesn't seem to make much headway,' Emily wrote to Clara. 'She is a silly little person, will not have got almost any pleasure out of her two years, when she might have got so much... If you live in the Nile it's wise to make friends with the crocodiles.' By 1913 she had become almost morbid. On hearing of her brother Alfred's death she wrote to Clara, 'I only wish I had been taken instead of him. I don't feel I'm much use in the world and could have been better spared.' Nevertheless, she stayed in India until the spring of 1914 when she came back to England for good.

Marion was the last of the aunts to enter my life and I was about six when she came back from the Canaries. At first I did not take to her at all. She was very tall, very upright, and appeared to me stern and rather formidable. Her nursing career had accustomed her to giving orders and she had an air of authority which I found a little forbidding. My first clear memory of this new aunt is of a fine warm day when she and Clara took me to the seaside at Alnmouth. This entailed a train journey of half an hour to Alnwick, then another short run to Alnmouth where the station was quite a long walk from the village and the beach. Of the outward journey and the hours we spent on the sands I have no recollection. What I do remember vividly is the trek back to Alnmouth station – a long, dusty road, a hot sun and two tired little feet. I tried to keep up with the aunts but they walked too fast. I lagged behind, they waited for me to catch up, then off they went again and once more I was left trailing in the rear. 'Come along, hinny, hurry up,' said Marion sharply. I trotted on again but there seemed no end to that road and the aunts <u>would</u> walk so fast. Marion lost patience. 'Will you <u>please</u> stop dawdling and keep up with us,' she ordered. I was near to tears and decided that I didn't like this aunt one little bit. Then Clara, bless her heart, said gently 'Darling, we don't want to hurry you, we know you're tired, but we don't want to miss the train do we?' So I trudged on and we did catch the train – by the skin of our teeth. Let me say at once that my first childish impression of Marion was utterly wrong, and it did not take me long to discover my mistake. No one ever had a kinder heart and I very soon came to love her dearly. In later years I owed to her kindness and understanding a debt of gratitude that could never be repaid.

None of the aunts could lay claim to good looks, but they had character and a charm and intelligence that were worth far more than physical beauty. On one occasion they had staying with them a cousin who was noted for her forthright speech, and one evening, when they were all sitting round the fire the cousin looked at each one in turn and remarked:

'I always felt <u>so</u> sorry for your poor mother.'
'Oh! Why?' asked the aunts.
'To have had five such <u>plain</u> daughters.'

To her great surprise this sally was greeted with gales of laughter from the aunts who had no illusions about their looks.

They had little clothes sense. They would often choose quite pretty dresses and ruin them by dragging them tightly up to the neck with a brooch and festooning themselves with beads or bits of lace. Nevertheless, they always looked neat when they went out and, however old-fashioned their clothes might be, they had a presence that outweighed any sartorial shortcomings. The Miss Robertsons were 'somebodies'.

Chapter III

A CHARM OF UNCLES

'I am a lone lom creetur... and everythink goes contrairy with me'
Charles Dickens: David Copperfield

A Charm of Uncles

Of uncles the only one of whom I have any clear recollection in my very early years is Jack, for Alfred was still in Canada, Conrad in Birmingham. When Jack returned from the South African war he stayed at home for a little while, for the sake of his widowed mother, but he could not settle and in March 1902, he went back to Canada. Though he was devoted to Elizabeth, and had great affection for all his brothers and sisters, he did not share their passionate love of Glanton. Just before he left home he wrote to Emily:

I shall be sorry to leave Glanton – not so much on my own account, though I must confess to a kindly regard for the place in spite of its deadly dullness, especially in the winter season – but somehow I think Mother will realise her lonely position much more keenly after I am gone. For a while, at least, but I trust that, under the cheerful influence of Spring and sunshine, she will find her lot easier to bear... I am looking forward to seeing the Great Unfenced again, and the bronchos and the Boys of the Old Brigade, and the Rockies, and feeling the subtle and indescribable charm of the Great West, which draws a man back to it in spite of …'

(The rest of the letter is missing.)

Elizabeth did feel bereft when Jack had gone, though she would never have tried to keep him at home when he wanted to go.

> *'It was indeed a sad, sad day,' she wrote to Emily. 'It was a hard parting... At Newcastle Uncle Conrad was waiting, and at parting put an envelope into his hand with £20 in it... Aunt Ann gave him £20 and is sending another £30... Oh, what a dull house it will be without him. It brings back all the old sorrow and we shall feel terribly the want of a manly step about, and a strong one to lean upon. Yet I cannot but feel grateful, very, that Jack has been able and willing to stay with us for so long.'*

This time Jack was farming on a ranch of his own - 'Bachelor's Hall,' he called it. Even his solitary spirit found it a lonely and depressing life, and, two years after his arrival at the ranch he wrote to Emily (who at this time was teaching the little girl who had enjoyed her 'frugal' tea):

> *'It is not so very bad when you get used to it. We read of prisoners who have come to love the cell in which they have been confined for many years. In fact one can get accustomed to anything, and I am now in that state when I take things as a matter of course... It certainly is a little slow at times, and the winter evenings drag somewhat, but there are breaks in the monotony. Every week I have visitors, policemen, cow-punchers and other wayfarers who look in, generally at midday, have a meal, praise my cookery and pass on. Then I have taken a holiday now and then... and though the place feels somewhat desolate and unhomelike when I return to it, the feeling wears off again... You cannot think how I am looking forward to Spring. The winters here are not severe, and this had been a particularly fine one so far, but I long for the time when the earth will be green again and the sun warm and the winds more kindly. Spring is such a <u>hopeful</u> time. I cannot*

say what is in store for me except hard work, but I hope and expect to leave this place, which I like very much in many ways – it is very suitable and has many natural beauties of its own – but which will ever be associated in my mind with long weary lonesome days and many disappointments. I hardly expect to find another where everything necessary is so handy – water, fuel, and suchlike – but I shall gladly take a less favourable "location" where one can have the society of his fellowmen. I am not cut out for a hermit's cell... I am "setting" bread tonight. Does not that simple statement bring before you very clearly my present mode of life? It is an epitome of bachelordom. It suggests cooking in all its branches, washing, mending, and all the other details of exemplary housekeeping – for Man, even lonesome man, cannot live on bread alone. He must branch out into the byways of cookery, peel potatoes, clean rabbits and fry the festive rasher. As a consequence, he must wash dishes, and other rags, which last, being rags, must needs be repaired, however clumsily, else will the wearer be unable to withstand the rigours of the winter. How sick and tired I am of all this, and when you consider that I am getting near the 40 mark it is not to be wondered at. O! That I could take mine ease in mine inn, which being interpreted means, O! That I had a real home of my own. But Poverty and perhaps also Prudence bar the way, and make travelling slow, so it may be that I shall not reach the inn by nightfall, but must camp as best I may by the roadside after all.'

He recalled the days at Glanton House when they were children:

'Saturdays and Sundays are all on one dead level nowadays, but I remember when Saturday night used to be an "occasion", a definite halting place on the onward march. You know in times long past it used to be bath night, then it came to be signalised as the night when the weekly paper came in. In later years, when the workaday world claimed us as its slaves, it brought with it the prospect of a day of rest on the morrow. But in this land Sunday has no special significance as a day of rest – to the rancher, at least. He may have to ride fast and far, or it may be only one of many days of enforced idleness. I generally <u>shave</u> on Sunday, however, if I have not lost count of the days of the week.'

Jack was going through a very difficult time; it seemed nothing would go right for him:

> *'One of my heifers had a calf this morning, but the young thing died soon after it was born – so does ill-luck pursue me. My friends leave me, my place I cannot hold, my dogs get poisoned, my cattle stray away and my calves die. I am a modern Job, without his exasperating patience. I hope better fortune may be in store for me after I leave this ill-starved place.'*

Poor Jack! He had started his letter on a reasonably cheerful, or at least resigned, note but writing to his favourite sister and recalling the happy days of the past had brought home to him the dreariness and loss of companionship that his present mode of life entailed. He had reached his nadir, and felt that he was wasting his life.

> *'This place, when the lamp is lighted and the world shut out, gives me the blues sometimes. I wonder what I am doing here, and why I have buried myself. It is such an unnatural sort of existence and quite unnecessary. I read until my eyes get tired sometimes, then I strum the banjo, but that instrument has no charms for me. I have nearly forgotten how to play it, and the old times have gone from me and no new ones take their place. For company I still have my two cats, which are at this moment curled up together on my bed. They are grey, and so much alike that I can hardly tell which is which. They tell me Ching (a Siamese) still lords it at Glanton, and is fat and flourishing. I think a cat has a real good time in most houses, and, if there is anything in the transmigration of souls, I should not mind being Ching in the future state.'*

Jack had had bad news, too, of his brother Alfred, who was still in Canada. It is not known what Alfred was doing at this time, but he had been compelled to 'put up his shutters' as business did not come his way and he had lost on the transaction.

> *'The fact is,'* Jack wrote, *'the Robertsons of the Glanton branch, and some of the other branches also, have not the necessary business capacity. It is not in them. Anyone of our name making*

a success of anything is unheard of... Will seems to have the fairest prospects of any of us, but no doubt he finds it a struggle to make headway.'

This was written in 1904, and it was not long after that Jack returned to England. When I was a small child I was rather in awe of him – he was well over six feet and had a gruff manner that concealed an intense shyness – but I was fond of him too and liked to 'help' him in the garden. He spent five years at home but, as always, the two sides of his nature were at war. When abroad he thought nostalgically of Glanton but, when at home, he became restless. The humdrum life of the village could not satisfy him for long and, in March 1909, he was once again off on his travels this time bound for Gisborne in New Zealand. But, in less than two years, he was home again.

Alfred had come to England for a short holiday in 1907 – the first time he had been home since he went to Canada in 1896 – but I have no recollection of this visit. Three years later he became engaged to a Canadian girl, Mary Munro, who was a violinist and lived in Regina.

Alfred and Mary 4th June, 1912

119

They were married there on 4th June, 1912, and came to England for their honeymoon. Mary was a very pretty girl with a mop of dark curls and I became greatly attached to her and to her quiet, gentle husband. Jack was at home at the time, Conrad came for his annual holiday and Will paid a flying visit to Glanton so that the four brothers might be together for the first time since 1896.

Just after Christmas Mary left their home in Winnipeg to spend a few days with her parents in Regina. She was never to see her husband alive again. On New Year's Eve, Alfred went out without a coat or any other protection against the bitter cold, and was found dead in the snow. The

Fateful telegram from Jack

reason for this strange behaviour was never fully explained. He had lived in Canada for years and well knew the dangers of exposure. He had apparently been in good health but had had one or two odd lapses of memory and it was thought that he had had a cerebral embolism. So died the first of the younger generation; he was only thirty-five.

Of Conrad I have only a very hazy recollection in the early days, probably because his holidays did not often coincide with ours.

Chapter IV

A GREAT LADY

'She was a worthy woman al her lyve'
Chaucer: *Prologue to the Canterbury Tales*

Aunts and uncles came and went, but there was one person who was always there, the presiding genius of Glanton House – my grandmother Elizabeth. When I first remember her she was only in her early sixties but to me she was always an old lady. Even before William's death, she had worn nothing but sombre colours for many a year for bright colours were only for the young, and youth ended in the twenties in Elizabeth's young days. She might wear a mauve or grey dress in the morning but after lunch she changed into 'her black', with a fichu* of lace over her shoulders, and always wore a lace or muslin cap. When she went out she wore a black coat or cape and a bonnet. Although she lived until 1922, she never changed her style of dress or hair-dressing. Her skirts remained full and ankle-length, her hair was still parted in the middle and draped low over her forehead as when William had first met her, and she carried her offertory to church in a little black reticule embroidered with black and white beads. Yet this adherence to the fashions of a bygone age never seemed incongruous. Like the late Queen Mary's hats, Elizabeth's clothes were an essential part of her image, and an expression of her personality; no one would have wanted her to make the slightest change.

She had had a hard life in many ways. She had borne eleven children and reared nine of them, and never in all their married life together were she and William free from financial worry. Yet none of this seemed to have left its mark. She was always serene, always sweet-tempered, wise and understanding, with a quiet but keen sense of humour. For more than sixty years she was the guiding spirit, the lode-star to whom all the family turned, and even when they had all gone out into the world, she was still the greatest influence in their lives.

It was my grandmother who first took me to church, and for many years I preferred the Presbyterian service to that of the Church of England.

---

* *A large square kerchief, folded into a triangle, worn around the shoulders and fastened at the front.*

For one thing, there was a very short 'sermon' for children followed by a children's hymn, and this was something to look forward to during the long prayers that preceded it, and to sustain one during the seemingly endless sermon for the grown-ups that followed. Then on the way home there was the thrill of collecting the post, for even this remote village had a Sunday post in those days. There was no delivery but the post office opened for a short time for letters to be called for and I was allowed to run ahead to perform this exciting duty.

Sunday afternoons were rather boring unless my father was there when he and I would go for a walk. Otherwise, I would bury myself in a book and, unlike the older generation, I was not restricted to 'good' books. But there was no one to talk to. Everyone except me went to sleep and wherever one went one came across a slumbering aunt or uncle. Two would occupy the armchairs in the dining-room (generally sharing with a cat or dog), another would retire to the drawing-room sofa and, on a fine day, one or two might be found asleep in deck chairs in the garden. The rest retired to their beds. Elizabeth was broad-minded as regards Sunday observance and was quite happy for me to play games, though she did not like the grown-ups to play tennis on the Sabbath. She would not have demurred if any of the family had wished to play but no one ever suggested it. It was her house and her wishes were respected. When, in later years, Will had a car, he knew that his mother did not approve of joy-riding on Sundays so the car was never brought out except, occasionally, to take us to the Anglican church in a neighbouring village. (Although brought up as a Presbyterian, Will, like his brother Jack, did not care for the service and became a member of the Church of England.) To use the car for church-going was quite permissible and, it must be confessed, that on a fine day we would sometimes come home by a rather roundabout route to get a little drive without hurting Elizabeth's sensibilities.

On weekdays she loved to be taken out in the car, her greatest joy being a picnic among the Cheviots which had been beyond her reach since William's death. Her favourite spot was a quite valley at the foot of a hill called the Glidders, beside the little river Breamish. The stream was very shallow and stony, and paddling was agony without rope-soled shoes, but there was a small pool deep enough for bathing so the younger members of the family, having undressed in the thick bracken, would disport

Paddling in the Breamish

themselves into the ice-cold water. On one occasion Elizabeth grew tired of being an onlooker so she borrowed a pair of bathing shoes, hitched up her skirts and joined the paddlers – still wearing her black coat and bonnet.

She loved her garden and, until nearly the end of her life, she took charge of the flower beds in front of the house and kept them immaculate. Another of her special preserves was the Pansy Walk. One of the long paths in the walled garden was grassed over and here Elizabeth planted a border of pansies on either side, a glorious sight in the summer. When she died Clara took over this task and kept the borders as her mother would have wished for many years.

Though always calm and unhurried, Elizabeth was never idle. She was a great reader but always, as she read, her knitting needles would be clicking and she kept all her sons supplied with socks. She was also a beautiful needlewoman and equally skilled at crochet. All her daughters inherited her gift for handicrafts, each with her own speciality. Emily took up leather-work and had a work-table on the attic landing. Later she worked with pewter and vellum, and whatever she did was of first-class quality and workmanship. Clara, like her mother, was a superb needlewoman. She made beautiful underwear (every stitch worked by hand for she scorned the machine), and she also made the finest lace – all by the light of the oil-lamp. Then she took up china painting, for which she always used the best bone china. Florence and Ina concentrated mainly on knitting, though Florence also did poker-work. After her mother's death, she bought herself a machine for knitting socks on which, after many hours of frustration before she mastered its vagaries, she turned out hosiery at a tremendous speed. Marion, too, was a knitter but she was also a keen dress-maker. She, however, preferred the machine to hand-sewing and, as unlike her sisters, she was not addicted to an outdoor life,

Elizabeth
Hands never idle

she would spend hours rattling away on the sewing machine even when the sun was shining and everyone else was spending every free moment in the open air. In Will and Jack, the gift for handwork expressed itself in carpentry. Jack made walking sticks, picture frames and other useful articles from odd branches cut from trees in the garden. He also painted very attractive water-colours, though he never had a painting lesson in his life.

CHAPTER V

SAND-CASTLES AND OTHER CASTLES

'Thy tower, proud Bamburgh, marked they there,
King Ida's castle, huge and square'
Scott: Marmion

On the coast, about twenty-five miles from Glanton, lies Bamburgh, once the proud capital of Saxon Northumbria, now just a small village. From the main street one catches a glimpse of the great castle, considerably restored but still retaining the original Norman keep and part of the walls. Although by the Middle Ages Bamburgh was no longer important as a town, the castle was still a strategic point. Whoever held Bamburgh, and its neighbours Dunstanburgh and Warkworth, commanded the north-east coast, and many bloody battles were fought there up to the time of the Wars of the Roses. Four hundred years later Bamburgh again achieved fame as the birthplace of Grace Darling, whose massive but ugly monument stands in the churchyard.

From the village street a lane called the Wynding leads to the dunes and the magnificent sandy beach, at one end of which the castle on its rock juts out into the sea. The sands are a paradise for children, shelving so gently that even the little ones can paddle safely, and among the limpet-encrusted rocks are delightful little pools where the tiniest toddlers can play happily.

In this delectable spot my parents and I spent a week of our holiday every year during my childhood, and I enjoyed many thrilling hours building sand-castles until one day my father suggested making a baker's shop, using a tin lid for the cakes. That was much more fun, and I firmly made up my mind that when I grew up I would be a baker.

When I was very small my parents made friends with a family called Davis who owned a little yacht, Vidette, and more than once they kindly put her at our disposal. With her skipper, Jim, we made several trips to the Farne Islands, with their fascinating names – the Wideopens, the Knoxes, the Walmses, the Brownsman – and to the Longstone, with its lighthouse from which Grace Darling and her father made their heroic journey to the wreck of the Forfarshire in 1838. To Will, who had not been to sea since his days as ship's surgeon, it was a great joy to feel a deck under his feet again, small though it was compared with the liners in which he had travelled to South Africa. Vidette boasted only twenty-eight tons, but she was a ship. This was my first experience of sea travel, and awakened in me the love of the sea and ships which I have inherited from my father.

The islands are teeming with bird-life – cormorants, gannets, kittiwakes and those clowns of the sea, the puffins – and one had to walk warily to avoid stepping on terns' eggs laid casually all over the ground, or their chicks, so wonderfully camouflaged that they were almost indistinguishable from the sand and single.

But my earliest recollection of Bamburgh is not of Vidette or of the Farne Islands, or even of the fun I had on the beach. It is of an incident that occurred in 1908, when I was only four, but which remains vividly in my memory. We were staying, as usual, at the Victoria Hotel, and at the next table in the dining-room (but they called it the coffee-room then), was a five-year-old boy with his father. One day at lunch, our parents amused themselves by asking their offspring the dates of famous battles.

'When was the battle of Trafalgar?' asked my father.

'1805,' I replied promptly, feeling very pleased with myself.

'And what was the date of Waterloo?' the little boy's father asked.

The question was addressed to me, not to his son. There was a dreadful silence, I didn't know. Even now, nearly seventy years later, I can still recall my shame and embarrassment, and my flaming cheeks, as I hung my head in confusion. But worse was to come.

'I know,' said the little boy brightly. '1815.'

My mortification was complete. Perhaps I should have felt less humiliated had I known that this infant prodigy would one day become Prime Minister. His name was Alec Douglas-Home.

Chapter VI

RANDOM RECOLLECTIONS

'Life went a-maying
With Nature, Hope, and Poesy

When I was young'
Coleridge: Youth and Age

(i)

At a very early age I had literary ambitions, and tried my hand at poetry in the <u>Wordsworthian</u> style under such titles as <u>Clouds</u> and <u>Butterflies</u> and <u>Ode to Grannie on her Birthday</u>, these masterpieces have passed into oblivion, and only <u>The Stars</u> survives:

'The little stars at night
Pour forth their shining light,
And make the darkness bright
As glorious day ......'

and so on for several verses. These effusions appeared to give great pleasure to Elizabeth and my aunts, who fondly looked upon me as a budding genius. Florence typed all my 'Poems' and bound them in a stiff cover of a fetching shade of pink. And I felt that I had really got into print. But I am afraid the family were doomed to disappointment, and personally I think it is as well I did not seriously aspire to becoming a poetess. The world is not much the poorer.

Unlike most children, I even enjoyed writing letters. There were, however, two occasions in the year when I did <u>not</u> like putting pen to paper – at Christmas and on my birthday – but I was brought up to write all the acknowledgements myself from the time when I first learned to make hieroglyphics that passed for letters. The real bugbear was Glanton, because I was expected to write a separate letter to Grannie and to each of the aunts, and to Jack if he happened to be at home – seven letters to people all living in the same house. The beginning was easy: 'Thank you for the - . I hope you had a happy Christmas.' That did for everyone, but then the trouble began. I would write a nice long newsy letter to Grannie, only to find that I had nothing left to say to anyone else. Then I devised a system. Before beginning my correspondence I wrote out a list of all the news items I could think of, and divided the result by the number of people at Glanton House. Any odd items remaining after the resolution of this mathematical problem were added to Grannie's letter, so that aunts and uncle were all treated alike.

The arrival of the Glanton parcel was one of the great excitements of the Christmas season. When I was a small child, Christmas posts might come at any hour of the day or evening, and often I was in bed when the Glanton parcel arrived. If it was not too late I was allowed to come downstairs to witness the unpacking of the outer wrappings, though the presents themselves must, of course, be kept until Christmas morning. As there were three of us and six or seven people at Glanton, there might be more than twenty packages, all beautifully wrapped in Christmas paper and tied with wide satin ribbon. If Jack was at home there was generally a hare which he had shot for us (that came separately, unwrapped, with a label tied round its hind legs), and always there was a large fruit cake know as the 'the Glanton leaf.' This was made from a recipe that had been handed down for generations, and each member of the family who was away from home received one at Christmas and on birthdays, even if it had to be sent to the other side of the world.

On one occasion Elizabeth sent me a lovely doll, all its clothes hand-made by herself. The dress was bright pink which, as she knew, was my favourite colour. Yet for some reason I disliked it at sight. 'Isn't this a beautiful doll your Grannie's sent you,' said my mother. 'I think it is perfectly horrid,' was my ungrateful reply. I always hated that doll. I called her Kathleen, and when I played 'schools' it was always Kathleen who was the naughty doll and smacked or put in the corner. Children's frankness can be very shattering. My cousin was once given a beautiful doll's house, furnished with loving care. It seemed to have everything that a little girl could desire, and her parents waited for her exclamations of delight. But all she said, after giving it the once-over in silence, was, 'Where's the lavatory?'

I always preferred teddy bears to dolls. One bear in particular – Bruno – was my inseparable companion for many years, and had been kissed so often that his nose became denuded of fur and had to be patched. He had his own miniature trunk, and an extensive wardrobe which included a suit of purple silk and a pair of pyjamas. When we acquired a car he, like the rest of us, wore a pair of goggles and a 'Burberry'.

(ii)

It was, I think, in 1910 or 1911 that I was wakened one day soon after sunrise, and accompanied Will and Dora and several aunts to the top of Glanton Hill. At six o'clock we opened the picnic basket and ate our breakfast, but always with one eye on the sky. It was one of the most exciting mornings of my young life. To be up so early, to be eating breakfast on the hillside, that was thrilling enough, but soon I should see something that none of us had ever seen before. What would it be like? Where should we look for it? We finished our meal, packed up the picnic basket, and settled down to wait, sitting in a circle so that every part of the landscape was under somebody's eye. We watched, we listened, but nothing disturbed the peace of the countryside. Hour after hour passed, and still we waited, still nothing happened. At ten o'clock we reluctantly abandoned our vigil. It wouldn't come now. Sad and deflated we made our way back to Glanton House.

At three o'clock that afternoon, when no one was about to see it, the aeroplane flew over Titlington Mount, within two miles of Glanton. It was taking part in an air race organized, I think, by one of the daily newspapers, but was several hours behind schedule. So ended the long awaited chance of seeing our first flying machine.

As late as 1916 Elizabeth thought it worth recording, in a letter to Clara, that she had 'had a sight of another aeroplane.' Only three years later Emily, the adventurous, wrote, 'Aren't you longing to go up in an aeroplane, Tim? I'd just give anything. I think it won't be long before many ride in the air.' Emily did not have to wait very long. During the 1920s she paid a brief visit to France, and flew back in a tiny aeroplane only big enough to hold her and the pilot. She enjoyed every minute of the flight. 'I felt like a bird,' she cried ecstatically, flapping her arms. She became the heroine of Glanton.

(iii)

One of the great characters of Glanton was a little old lady called Miss Hogg, who kept the village shop. She wore steel-rimmed

129

spectacles on the end of her nose, and looked like a beneficent owl. I was allowed to visit Miss Hogg by myself to buy sweets, and, although I had only threepence a week for pocket-money (of which a penny had to be kept for the church collection), one could buy quite a lot of sweets when acid drops and pear drops were a penny a quarter. (This was <u>old</u> pence, of course).

Another old lady who fascinated me was Bessie, who took in washing. She lived in a tiny cottage in the Playwell Lane, and the little room where she worked was always piled high with laundry, unbearably stuffy and smelling of warm damp woollens and hot irons. At whatever hour one visited her, she was always busy with her iron, enveloped in a cloud of steam. She had been doing this for so long that she was bent double, her chin permanently resting on her chest.

A familiar sight in the village was a woman who always wore red carpet slippers and seemed to spend most of her time weaving her way along the street with a large jug in her hand. In my innocence I thought it must contain milk, and wondered why she carried it up and down the road so often. Only when I was older, and understood the reason for her somewhat unsteady gait, did I connect her peregrinations with visits to the village inn.

Front Street, Glanton

Then there was the effeminate young man who always wore rubber soles and padded along as though he was treading on hot bricks. The villagers called him 'Little Flannel Foot.'

A walk up the village street was never dull.

One of the most exciting events in the aunts' calendar was gathering blaeberries. They looked forward to it for weeks, and when the great day came they put on their special blaeberrying clothes that were kept from year to year for this purpose. It was their contention that the operation could not be carried out without tearing one's clothes to ribbons and smothering oneself in fruit stains, though why it should cause more damage to one's habiliments than gathering any other fruit was never made clear. It is a pity that no one ever took a photograph of the party setting out on the annual expedition. Skirts held up with tape, blouses fastened together with safety-pins, laddered stockings, hats that had long lost any shape they might once have had – this was the regulation garb for blaeberry-picking. And the berries did not grow on the doorstep. This incredible cortege had to walk more than two miles to woods the other side of Whittingham. But what did it matter? In their own village everyone knew them, farther afield nobody knew them, so why should they worry?

As soon as I was old enough I was taken on this outing and it was impressed upon me that I was being given a great treat. I thought otherwise. Though I was too polite to say so, I hated every minute of it. In the first place, I disapproved of the aunts' costumes, and felt self-conscious walking up the village with them. This was not really snobbishness; it was merely a horror, shared by most young children, of being different. My mother always dressed well, and though at Glanton she wore clothes suitable for the country she was never anything but neat and well groomed. I felt that everyone must be staring at the aunts, and consequently at me as part of the procession, and this caused me great embarrassment. Of course, when I grew older I regarded the quaintness of the aunts' apparel with tolerance and affectionate amusement, and realised that no one in Glanton considered it at all odd. The Miss Robertsons were highly respected ladies, and what they wore was no one's concern but their own.

When we reached the woods I was given a pint-size milk can to fill. Anyone who has ever gathered blaeberries will sympathise with my feeling of utter hopelessness. The berries were so tiny, the can so large, and however conscientiously one picked one seemed to make no impression. The woods were pleasant enough, but they were the happy hunting ground of innumerable ravenous insects. There were midges that appeared in their cohorts to share our picnic lunch. They crawled up inside our clothes, so that by the end of the day we were all scratching like a band of monkeys. Then came the long walk home, uphill all the way.

'Hasn't it been a <u>lovely</u> day?' an aunt would say.
'Yes,' I would reply meekly.

But not even the delicious blaeberry pie that appeared on the lunch table next day could compensate for those hours of misery.

CHAPTER VII

THE HAZARDS OF THE ROAD

'Once there were velvet lads with vizards on their faces,
Riding up to rob me on the Great North Road …
Where are they flown then? Flown where I follow;
They are all gone for ever up the Great North Road'
Alfred Noyes: The Great North Road

In 1912 my father acquired his first car. Until then he had done all his visiting on foot or on his bicycle, and he was the first doctor in the neighbourhood to own a car. It was a second-hand Ivanhoe, an open tourer, square and box-like, dark blue with plenty of brass. It was Will's pride and joy, and he called it Angelina. As there was no accommodation for a car at our house, Angelina had to live in a garage a quarter of a mile away, and my father cycled there every morning to fetch her.

At week-ends we would often drive out into the country, sometimes taking one or two of my school friends, for a car drive was still a novelty and an excitement. In 1912 it did not take long to get out of London (the underground ended at Clapham Common), and when we had passed through Mitcham we were in rural surroundings. A favourite drive was to the little town of Sutton or the village of Carshalton. On one occasion Will took a wrong turning, and we were hopelessly lost. We found ourselves in a narrow lane which eventually led to the tiny and (to us) unheard of village – of Morden!

When the time approached for our annual visit to Glanton, Will had been driving Angelina for several months and she had behaved like a perfect lady. He spent many happy hours planning our first long journey – and three hundred miles was a very long journey then. The speed limit, even on major roads, was thirty miles an hour (not long before it had been twenty), and there were frequent police traps to catch the rash motorist who dared to risk life and limb by speeding at thirty-five miles an hour. The Automobile Association gave their members warning of these traps. Then one had to allow for mechanical breakdowns, which were all too common, and as punctures were almost inevitable on any long journey, we carried a goodly supply of spare outer tyres and inner tubes. We could not possibly cover three hundred miles in less than three days, Will decided, and we might not get further than Newark (125 miles) on the first day, though he hoped that with luck we might get as far as Retford or Bawtry. If all went <u>very</u> well, perhaps we could reach Doncaster – but no, that was too much to hope for; it was over 160 miles. Even in July and August there was no need to book hotel accommodation in advance, so our destination was left to Fate – and Angelina.

All wearing goggles, and my mother and I swathed in motoring veils, we set off at 7a.m. to escape the worst of the London traffic – mostly horse-drawn carts, bicycles and trams – and Angelina showed her mettle. Once we were clear of London she raced along the Great North Road at a merry thirty m.p.h. and fairly ate up the miles. Newark came and went, Retford was left behind, we sailed through Bawtry and arrived at Doncaster in plenty of time for dinner. We were more than halfway to Glanton in one day.

The next morning Will sent his mother a telegram saying that we should arrive that evening. All went well for two or three hours, and we expected to be at Glanton in time for tea. Suddenly Angelina made a horrible choking noise, spluttered once or twice, then dug in her toes and refused to move another yard. In vain did Will encourage her, cajole her, implore her; she had done her two hundred miles and she would go no further. A passing car took a message into Darlington, a breakdown truck arrived, and we were towed ignominiously to a garage. This was serious, they said; they could not possibly do the repairs in less than a week. A <u>week</u>! With our tails between our legs we sent another telegram to Glanton, went to a hotel in Darlington for the night and the following day finished the journey by train, clattering up to Glanton House in Foggin's wagonette as in days of yore.

A week later Will went back to Darlington by train to fetch Angelina. She had been put into some sort of working order, but the garage did not hold out much hope for her future. It seemed unwise to trust her to take us back to London, so, sad at heart, Will decided that he would have to part with the old lady. He arranged with a garage in Wooler to take her in part exchange for a brand-new Rover 12. This should have been exciting, but it wasn't. We didn't want a brand-new Rover, we wanted Angelina; but she had to go. When the day of parting came and I watched Will drive her away from Glanton House for the last time, it seemed to me like the end of the world. As she disappeared through the gate I fled to the far end of the garden and sobbed my heart out.

But even I had to admit that the new Rover was beautiful. She was light beige, long and sleek, far quieter and more comfortable than Angelina, and every few days we spent hours washing her and polishing her vast area of brass. She remained with us for fourteen years, and seldom gave any trouble. The only serious breakdown I remember was due to tyres, not to the car. It was during the First World War and again we were on our way to Glanton. The roads, full of marching troops, were littered with nails from their army boots. I don't know what effect it had on the boots, but for us it meant puncture after puncture. Garages were few and far between, and it was not easy to get tyres mended in a hurry, but we had started off with six spare tyres or inner tubes and there seemed no cause for worry. After the sixth puncture Will did feel slightly uneasy, but we had not much further to go, and once we reached Glanton .....

The seventh puncture occurred in the middle of Framlington Moor – only ten miles from Glanton but it might as well have been a hundred. We were out in the wilds, with no more spare tyres and no garage nearer than Morpeth, fourteen miles behind us. It was rapidly getting dark, for we had lost a great deal of time changing tyres, and there seemed to be no other travellers on the road that evening. At last we saw a lorry approaching and, to our relief, the driver stopped when he saw our frantic signals. He agreed to take Dora back to Morpeth for help, while Will and I waited with the car. The garage was shut when Dora arrived, but she banged on the door until the owner reluctantly opened it. Though she explained our dire predicament he refused to help. He had had a hard day's work, he said, and he was not prepared to turn out at that time of night. 'Oh, <u>please</u> come,' Dora begged. 'My husband and only child are out there all alone on the cold dark moor. You <u>must</u> help us.' But still he refused. Then Dora did the only possible thing; she burst into tears. She had, after all, been an actress. The tears did the trick. The garage proprietor was not proof against this display of feminine frailty, and he came to our rescue. With four good tyres – but still no spares – we reached Glanton without further mishap, to the great relief of the worried family, who had had visions of three mangled corpses lying in a mortuary.

Chapter VIII
TROUBLED TIMES

'When sorrows come, they come not single spies, but in battalions'
Shakespeare: <u>Hamlet</u>

(i)

Emily had spent several years at home after her father's death, but money was short, and in 1912 she decided to become a governess again. She had often wanted to revisit Germany, and in February of that year she spent a few months teaching in Dessau and Custrin, and staying with her old friend Olga, who had given her French lessons in the 1890s. But when spring came she pined for England and returned home in May.

At this time I was being taught by a rapid succession of not very competent governesses. As Emily needed a post, and was much better qualified than the young women who had so far been entrusted with my education, my parents asked her to take me on. She took a flat near us, and gave me lessons every morning. This appeared to be an excellent arrangement from everyone's point of view – except mine. I was very fond of her as an aunt, but as a governess she frightened me. She was impatient and quick-tempered, I was shy and often tongue-tied, afraid to answer her questions for fear of making a <u>gaffe</u> and incurring her wrath – or worse, her ridicule. Many a time I was reduced to tears by the end of the morning.

When she was telling me about the Great Plague and the Fire of London, I asked whether the plague had caused the fire. 'Of course not,' she replied, laughing, and later she told my parents of my foolish question. 'How superstitious children are!' she said. But it was not really superstition. My childish conception of the plague was, though I did not know it, that of many of its seventeenth century victims themselves – something caused by a miasma (though that word was not in my eight-year-old vocabulary). To my childish mind it seemed perfectly reasonable to think that this miasma might have led to spontaneous combustion, but I was quite incapable of explaining my theory, so I sat in embarrassed silence while I was dubbed superstitious and laughed at. This episode, and others like it, made me more reticent than ever, so poor Emily must have had a good deal to put up with; I cannot have been a very inspiring pupil. Nevertheless, she taught me more in the year I spent under her tuition than all the other governesses put together.

Even a year or two later, when I had gone to school, I was apparently still ridiculously shy. While I was at Glanton Emily wrote to Clara:

> *Joyce is – Joyce, canny and sweet, but painfully prim, and never speaking, can't even ask for the sugar or butter, it seems. She walks sedately and neatly to the picnics, always going out and coming in by the front door.'*

It would appear that, for some reason, it was considered slightly snobbish of me to use the front door instead of the back, but I had a motive for it. If I went through the kitchen where the aunts were working, I was often called upon to run errands, which interfered with my own more interesting pursuits. It was also regarded as affectation and urban-mindedness to walk up the village on the footpath; the aunts always walked in the middle of the road. Fortunately there was little motor traffic in those days, and a car gave ample warning of its approach by frequent blasts from its brass Klaxon horn as it rushed through the village at fifteen miles an hour.

(ii)

The summer of 1914 brought great trouble to the family. My parents and I went to Glanton in July, a month of glorious weather when even Northumberland enjoyed a heat wave. After spending a week there, Will and Dora went off for a few days on their own, leaving me at Glanton House. It was still very warm and sunny when they set off, but in the early evening the fine weather broke in a tremendous thunderstorm. I was in my bath when I saw a strange car drive up to the house. Wondering who the unexpected visitors might be I peered out of the window, and saw my mother, obviously in great distress, in a strange car and accompanied by a uniformed chauffeur. Where was my father? In a panic I jumped out of the bath and was about to rush downstairs, dripping and unclad, when Clara came to tell me what had happened.

Will and Dora had stopped for a picnic lunch on a lonely moorland road. For drinks they had taken bottles of soda water. In those days the bottles did not have caps; instead, a round piece of glass like a marble was wedged into the neck, and to open it one pushed the marble down into the bottle. The picnic basket had been on the luggage rack at the back of the car (there was no boot) and had become very hot. When Will pushed the marble, the bottle exploded in his face, and a splinter of glass lodged in his eye, which began to bleed profusely. He realized that he must get to a hospital as quickly as possible, but the nearest was in Hexham; twenty miles away. And Dora could not drive. Somehow, with blood pouring from his eye and in agonizing pain, Will made that journey, and was admitted for immediate operation. By this time not only had he lost a great deal of blood, but all the fluid had drained from the eye, leaving it quite flat.

Dora was not allowed to see her husband and, as there was no telephone at Glanton House, she hired a car and returned to Glanton to tell us what had happened. She crossed the moors while the storm was at its height. Forked lightning was flashing from the hillsides, and the torrential rain reduced visibility to almost nil. To Dora, who was terrified of thunderstorms at the best of times, the drive was a nightmare. Two days later she returned to Newcastle and stayed with friends of the Robertsons, so that she could visit Will in Hexham every day.

Will came through the operation well, but for more than a week he had to lie on his back and remain absolutely still. He said afterwards that the pain in his eye was nothing to the agony of being unable to move a muscle. The operation was successful, the eye returned to its normal shape, and his sight was little impaired – a remarkable feat of surgery for those days. Unfortunately the cure was not lasting; Will did eventually lose the sight of that eye, but it happened so gradually that he hardly noticed it. He had wonderful sight in his good eye to the end of his life, and when he was in his eighties he could still read a newspaper without his glasses.

While he was still in hospital Dora had a telegram telling her that her brother, John, was desperately ill with typhoid. Dora was distracted, torn between a desire to see her brother, who might be dying, and her reluctance to leave Will, but she felt that her first duty was to her husband, and she stayed in Northumberland until he was able to return to London. Fortunately John recovered.

(iii)

Then came the climax of this disastrous summer – the outbreak of the First World War. In the afternoon of 4th August I was playing in the garden when I heard distant gunfire, and I rushed into the house with my thrilling news. 'Nonsense,' said my elders. 'We're not at war yet.' But I was right; they <u>were</u> guns, fired from Tyneside, but it was not until the following morning that we heard that war had been declared, so long did news take to travel in those far-off days before the advent of domestic radio.

Many of the Glanton lads enlisted at once, but some, especially those working on the farms, were less eager to leave home. Anyway the war would be over by Christmas, we were told. One day a recruiting sergeant came to the village and persuaded a farmer's son to join up, but he then had to face the lad's mother. 'My son,' she said, 'has always had a good feather bed. Please see that he has one. <u>And</u> he is to be made a sergeant immediately.' The recruiting sergeant's reply is not on record.

The Robertsons were prompt to answer the call of 'King and Country.' Marion was the first to go. She had not gone back to hospital after her return from the Canaries, but had frequently taken jobs as private nurse in the neighbourhood. She was on the nursing reserve, and three days before war broke out she received her calling-up notice. She hastily packed her bag and went back to Manchester, where she was in charge of a military hospital all through the war. In 1917 she received a commendation from the War Office, the equivalent of 'mentioned in despatches.'

Florence decided that the most useful thing she could do was to stay where she was, and, as more and more of the male staff were called up, she assumed ever greater responsibility in Mr. Cooper's office.

Clara and Ina both volunteered for nursing, and the local branch of the Red Cross met in the kitchen of Glanton House, where they did a crash course of first aid and home nursing, frequently calling me in as a 'patient' for their bandaging practice. After her training, Clara went to

139

Newcastle, where Armstrong College had been turned into a hospital, the nurses sleeping in the Grand Hotel. Now that she was living in a city, her family inundated her with shopping orders, until she pointed out that, as she was on duty from morning to night, she had little opportunity of going to the shops. Early in 1915, however, she went on night duty, and immediately the family sent her commissions.

Nurse Clara

'Please get me 6 yds of narrow embroidery for the neck and sleeves of my combinations,' wrote Ina, 'and 2½yds of wide for legs. It need not be very good – what you think will wear out the combies and I do not care in the least about the pattern.'

By the same post her mother asked her to get two yards of silk.

'I got a blouse from the Glove Co. and think if I could make a deep basque or panniers – which I see are much worn – I could get a good deal of wear out of my old skirts.'

She also wanted wool for knitting socks. Emily soon added her requirements:

'You might get me, please, that blue tie if you see one – up to 1/6. That is a nice one Ina has, a kind of knitted one ..... Also two little tassels or bobbles for that bit of velvet.'

Poor Clara! One feels that her sleep and her leisure must have been sadly curtailed.

She endeared herself to the men she nursed in Newcastle, and received several letters from her former patients when they had been moved elsewhere. One, who had been sent to Hornsea, in Yorkshire, wrote:

Just a few lines hoping you are keeping in good health as it leaves me at present I am very bad with my chest now …. This is an awful place you can see nothing but the sea coast and the Hills you are about 21 miles from a town.'

Another had gone to Shotley Bridge, in Co. Durham, where Elizabeth had been born, and he, too, disapproved of his rural surroundings:

'Dear Nurse Just a few Lines hopping to find you well as it Leves me just about the same there is to many big Hills Bare for me to Clime Just yet but when I get here a bit Longer and a bit stronger I might mangange them all right you just walk from one Place to another all Day long but I will have to waite till I get a nice young Girl to show me about the Place And then i will be alright but i Do not think i will get manay Like yourself to be as good And kind to me you Have Being as good a friend a ever i Had so I will not Have to forget you when i get all Better and i Hope it will not Be Long And then i might stay in newcastle And see you more but I Hope i am not in Bad Health when i am there becase i think i Have Had Plenty of that God nows how Long i might Be here so I think That is all that Present From A Dear Friend Right Back soon And Let me no How you are getting on.'

In 1916 Clara was sent to France. She remained there for three years – at Le Treport, Etaples and Boulogne – and had several narrow escapes when these coastal towns were bombed. During all this time she had only one home leave.

Bracelet marking Clara's contribution to the Voluntary Aid Detachment and the British Expeditionary Force

Early in 1915 Ina went to Alnwick, where the Duchess's School had been taken over as a Hospital. At first she lived in the Castle with the Sisters, and enjoyed quite a luxurious life: 'a room to myself with a fire and a bath brought into my bedroom and hot water ad lib brought in by the maid who waits on us, and every comfort.' But this was too good to last, and soon she was living in a hut. After a few months she was transferred to Howick Hall, near Dunstanburgh, the ancestral home of a branch of the Grey family – an association which pleased the Robertsons, who were all staunch Liberals and great admirers of the Foreign Secretary, Lord Grey of Falloden. Then, in July, 1916, Callaly Castle, a mansion only a few miles from Glanton, was opened as a military hospital, and Ina took up duty there.

The first few days at Callaly were chaotic. The ladies in charge had been told to expect fourteen patients, but at four o'clock on the previous afternoon they received a telegram telling them that there would be twenty-eight. The supplies of food were hopelessly inadequate, the Matron had not yet arrived, nor had the extra kitchen staff. Marion happened to be home on leave, and was roped in to bring order out of chaos in the wards, while Emily went to help in the kitchen. For some time Emily had felt that she should take some active part in the war effort, and had thought of volunteering for munition work. The difficulty was that there was no munitions factory near Glanton and, with all her sisters away, she did not feel that she could leave her mother. She was sure she would never make a good nurse (she was probably right), but one thing she could do was cook. Callaly offered the perfect solution. Instead of going there for only one day, she stayed on as part-time cook during the whole of the hospital's short life. She went for a week at a time, then Ina for a fortnight, so that Elizabeth was never left alone.

Unfortunately Callaly was closed in October, 1917, after only eighteen months' existence. Emily was sorry that her war work had come to an end, but Ina was even more distressed, and became quite miserable as the closing date drew near.

> 'She's that glued to Callaly,' Emily wrote to Clara, 'she'd never come home at all if she could help it … she certainly does not add to the general hilarity. She is mournful and depressed and takes herself very seriously, dresses like a lovelorn orphan, and speaks

*with difficulty and often talks Tamil, a most depressing language,
I think ... Yet at Callaly, apparently, she is the moving spirit.'*

Even Marion, who adored her younger sister, could not refrain from comment when writing to Clara:

*'She is amusing! I, I, is never off her tongue – she runs Callaly
and rules the men, and the whole thing would have fallen in
ruins if it were not for her – according to her! She is quite the
most important personage there. It really is funny, she takes
herself very seriously.'*

It is easy, with hindsight, to understand Ina's self-importance. As the youngest girl she had always been treated as a baby. She was never given any responsibility in the running of the house, but was at the beck and call of her elder sisters. In the days when there was a maid in the kitchen it was Ina who was told to ring the bell. If something was wanted from the village shop it was Ina who was told to 'run up and fetch it.' Nearly forty years later Emily said to me, 'I'm too old to wear short-sleeved dresses now, but of course Ina can,' Ina being then a mere child of 75 to Emily's 85! Now at Callaly for the first time in her life Ina was a person in her own right, someone upon whom others depended, no longer merely a shadow of her more forceful sisters, but this they did not understand. She had also become genuinely fond of nursing, and had no intention of giving it up when Callaly closed. After a short period at Long Horsley, not far from Glanton, she went to a hospital at Dunstan-on-Tyne. This carried on after the war as an after-care hospital for service patients, and so much did Ina enjoy working there that she stayed until 1924.

CHAPTER IX

THE WAR DRAGS ON

'The men that worked for England'
G.K.Chesterton: Ecclesiastes

(i)

When war broke out Jack was already over military age, but, as was to be expected, he was only too anxious to break away from the monotony of life at Glanton. By falsifying his age he managed to get into the army immediately and, in view no doubt of his experience with the North-West Mounted Police, was posted to a remount depot in France. This was the perfect job for him, and he spent most of the war looking after the horses at the depot and taking them up to the Front as required. He had enlisted as a private, and firmly refused all offers of a commission. He liked the personal contact with horses, and feared that as an officer he would become involved in administrative work, which was distasteful to him. One could, however, have too much of a good thing. In August, 1915, he wrote to Emily:

'Here at the Base it is horses, horses, horses, from morning to night, seven days a week. The horse is undoubtedly an interesting animal, and loveable enough, but to tell the truth I would like kangaroos or ostriches for a change. The best work is exercising. It takes us out of Camp, and along the beautiful lanes which abound hereabouts…There is a lot of corn grown ….There will be no famine in this land if the Germans are kept out of it … Never a young man do we see, only women and children and old peasants, who have perhaps done their bit in the sad days of '70.'

As always when he was away from home, Jack longed for Glanton, and in June, 1915 he wrote to Clara:

'Anyone who knows Glanton in June would wish to be there of all places in the world just now, and its associations are so very dear that at all times it is the one spot on earth for all of us.'

A year later he wrote to Ina:

'Glanton is never very long out of my thoughts, for that is where my heart is, and I long for a sight of the old place.'

He was amused by the modern fashions of the girls at the depot:

'The young women – for one must call them all young, I suppose – the <u>young</u> women who work in this camp are very up to date in some ways. They have a stride and swing of the arms which are distinctly masculine. Some have their hair cut short.'

The 'bob' had just become fashionable.

His mother and sisters seemed to imagine that he was living in a tent, was permanently suffering from cold, and tore his underclothes to shreds. Every week or two he received a parcel of woollen garments, and was hard put to it to store them all in his limited hut accommodation. In vain did he assure his loving family that his supplies were more than adequate; still the woollies came. It was several months before he convinced them and the flow of underwear came to an end.

During the last summer of the war Jack's depot suffered from a plague of flies, and he wrote an amusing letter to Ina headed 'Fly Time,' decorated on every page with life-size drawings of the pestiferous insects:

'Here we get dust and flies. I've not seen so many flies since I was at Gisborne, N.Z. That place certainly took the cake, or rather flies took it, and everything else of an edible nature…. The pests are crawling over my hands as I write, and investigating the contents of the inkpot if haply it may contain jam, such as they batten on in the mess room.'

By now there was a shortage of horses, and Jack was enjoying a new experience.

'Do you know anything about mules? I am learning something every day, for it is mules, mules, mules, all day and every day, with me, riding them (without a saddle), grooming and feeding them, fighting and petting them, cursing and caressing them. For there are mules and mules. I am looking forward to the day when

145

their services will be required at the Front, and their voices make musical the plains of Flanders and Picardy.'

Jack had home leave in the autumn of 1916, then did not see Glanton again until after the armistice.

(ii)

Will was too old to join the forces, and carried on in his London practice, but he joined the local Defence Volunteers. He also became medical officer in charge of Clapham Road (later Clapham North) underground station during air raids. In the absence of special shelters hundreds of people repaired to the nearest underground when the warning maroons went off, and, as Clapham Road station was at the end of our road, we would watch the pathetic human stream passing our house carrying babies, cats and dogs, bird-cages and cooking utensils, prepared to make a night of it. Will was told that he could either join this crowd and stay in the station until the 'All Clear' was sounded, or risk walking down the road in the middle of an air raid if his services were required – and he would not be given a 'tin hat'. He could think of nothing worse than being cooped up with this seething mass of humanity for perhaps several hours, and he had his own patients to consider, so he chose the second alternative. In fact he was never called to the station.

During the earlier raids, when only Zeppelins were used, it did not occur to us to seek shelter in the basement. Instead, we all repaired to the attic of our five-storey house, whence we had a grandstand view of the great lumbering airships caught in the searchlights, with shells bursting all round them. They were so huge, so slow, that one wondered how they could possibly escape the London barrage. Once we did see one hit. It wobbled, its nose dipped then it continued unsteadily on its way, eventually crashing in Surrey beyond our range of vision. A great cheer went up from the crowd in the street. Not long after, we heard the welcome sound of the 'All Clear,' a bugle blown by Boy Scouts on bicycles.

In 1915 Will was still able to take his car to Glanton, and one day he took Ina and two young girls from the village to Alnwick. 'Will drove very fast in places,' Ina told Clara, '40 m.p.h., and the girls were very delighted and squealed with pleasure or apprehension.' But in 1916 no petrol was available, and once again we had to make the journey by train. This grieved Will, less for his own sake than for that of his mother, who so greatly enjoyed her drives with him. In 1917, however, he was asked by a doctor in Alnwick to act as locum while the doctor and his family went on holiday. They were taking their car with them and, as it was impossible for Will to run a scattered country practice without one and car-hire had not then been thought of in Alnwick, he was granted a special allowance of petrol for the purpose. As several of the patients lived in or near Glanton, Will was able to take Elizabeth with him on some of his rounds.

During our journey back to London Will lost his way in a town and stopped to ask a policeman. We were about to drive on when the policeman put his head inside the window and enquired:

> 'May I ask, sir, for what purpose you are using your car?'
> 'I'm a doctor,' Will replied.
> 'That's quite all right, sir,' said the policeman, and waved us on.

Will's reply was genuine enough, but nothing could have looked less like a doctor's car on professional business than did our car at that moment. A doctor might well take his wife with him, but there were, in addition, a thirteen-year-old child, an Australian officer who had been staying at Glanton, a Pomeranian dog, a pile of cases on the luggage rack, a picnic basket and several cameras. That policeman had a trusting soul – or perhaps Will had an honest face.

(iii)

Meanwhile Elizabeth was not idle. She played her part in the war effort by knitting harder than ever, turning out dozens of pairs of socks, Balaclava helmets and bedsocks for the troops. Every summer her cousin, Carrie Dixon, came to Glanton for several months, and she too was a great knitter. Jack could imagine how busy the two old ladies would be:

> 'I am sure Carrie's fingers will be busy at some work for soldiers.

Can't you picture her and Mother going at it for all they are worth, every night, with fingers that never seemed to tire. How I used to wish they would stop sometimes to <u>rest</u>. I'm sure I showed them a good example from the depths of the big armchair.'

It was at this time that Elizabeth taught me to knit. She decided that bedsocks would be easiest for a beginner, and gave me the money to buy the wool at the village shop. She must have been a little disconcerted by my choice of colour – bright scarlet – but she did not bat an eyelid. 'A nice cheerful colour,' she said. I took to knitting like a duck to water and the bedsocks grew apace; so much did they grow that by the time I had cast off the feet were about fifteen inches long and broad in proportion. The bedsocks were sent to Marion in Manchester, and with great tact she told me that she had given them to an Australian soldier who had <u>very</u> big feet and was delighted with them.

In the early days of the war Glanton suffered little from food shortages. At the beginning of 1915 Elizabeth was able to buy two large chickens for five shillings the pair, and when we went there in the summer we lived on the fat of the land. But gradually even Glanton came to feel the pinch, and prices soared. In 1917 Elizabeth said that she would have to give up knitting large garments, because wool was 6s 10d a pound. Nine months later it had gone up to 8s. Eggs rose to 3d each, and butter was 2s 2d a pound. Potatoes, which were unobtainable in London at any price – we used rice instead – were 2s a stone in Alnwick, but Elizabeth managed to get some at 1s 4d a stone, 'and generally at this time of year they are 4d or 5d,' she said. All the Robertsons were great sugar eaters, even piling it on jam and treacle puddings (but never on porridge, of course) and when, at the end of 1917, sugar rationing was introduced, somewhat belatedly, Ina wrote to Clara:

'I do not know how we will manage when the sugar cards come out. It seems impossible to make ½lb a week do. That is 1oz per day with 1oz per week over for cooking. Mother takes an ounce in her coffee morning and evening alone and we must not reduce that whatever happens.'

In November, 1917, Elizabeth wrote to Clara:

148

'We at home are feeling the effects of War – it will be a queer Xmas. Xmas puddings, mince meat and loaves [fruit cakes] will be scarce. We have not been able to get a currant for a long time, butter is unthinkable – all the hens in the country seem to have gone on strike, no eggs to be had. There was not a bit of bacon in all the shops in Alnwick last week, and when it is to be had is 2/2 the lb ....Tea too is scarcely to be had. Shops are selling only 2oz at a time, and 4/- a lb.'

But clothes could still be made cheaply with local labour. The girls had clubbed together to give their mother a dress, and Emily told Clara:

'It is very pretty and nicely made ...and <u>very</u> cheap, only 10/- for the making. The trimmings, linings, etc. with making came to £1 8 0 ...It is nice material, 6/- per yard.'

When one considers the amount of material needed for Elizabeth's full skirts, it was cheap indeed!

Meanwhile wages, too, were rising, and Elizabeth was amazed to hear that quite a young girl who worked in the General Post Office earned 25s a week with lunch and tea. One of the Barber girls, in her first job, was earning 40s a week, and her elder sister even had to pay income tax!

Glanton did not escape the spy phobia that swept the country during the early days of the war. Ina told Clara that two evangelists who were holding meetings in the district – quite harmless and well-meaning characters, no doubt – were said to be German spies, and had been hissed out of the village.

During the war the trees on Thrunton Crag, the wooded hill that provided the background to the lovely view of Whittingham Vale from Glanton House were cut down. The first foresters were Finns, and it was while they were there that there was a forest fire which, while by their standards probably of minor proportions, was spectacular and rather terrifying when viewed from the bottom of the Glanton House garden. Then came the Canadians, and their impact was more far-reaching than mere deforestation, for they carried off many of the Northumbrian maidens. Several Glanton girls married Canadian soldiers, including Hannah, the faithful maid. Most of them left their native village for ever, but Hannah did come back to Glanton for a holiday. It was many years later, when I was grown up, and I hardly recognized in this charming, smartly dressed middle-aged woman the young girl whom I remembered in a black dress and cap and apron in my childhood. But Hannah had not really changed, and her Canadian accent had not destroyed her native Northumbrian burr. Her visit gave great pleasure to the Robertsons to whom she had been such a good friend in days long past.

The current 'help' had a brother in France, and announced proudly that he had been 'larnin' French,' but it had taken him a whole month to 'get perfect.' Emily, reporting this achievement to Clara, also in France, said, 'Tim, I'm afraid you're very slow!' It was the same girl's mother who, admiring Elizabeth's magnificent geraniums, remarked, 'By, but geraniums is tarble flooers for flooerin'.'

Even during the war, when travelling was difficult and uncomfortable, Florence always came home for Christmas. In 1916 she had an unusually unpleasant journey when the train, without warning, sailed through Alnmouth and carried her on to Chathill, many miles further north. She managed to catch a train back to Alnmouth, but arrived there too late for the Glanton connections, 'so,' Elizabeth wrote to Clara, 'the plucky little woman left her big luggage to come on by train, and walked up …We have had a tremendous frost – not one like it for years – and the roads were like glass, so you may imagine her trudge carrying a good heavy bag.' Another example of little Florence's grit and determination – but one does wonder why she brought so much luggage just for Christmas!

There was one event that brought great joy to Glanton House during the last trying year of the war. In May, 1918, a son was born to Conrad and his wife. 'Con … sent two snapshots of the boy.' Elizabeth wrote to Ina. 'He looks a little butter lump. He is a great crier and Con dwells upon his good lungs.' It would seem that my cousin resembled me in both size and yelling capacity.

Chapter X

BETWEEN THE WARS

'Peace is come, and wars are over'
A.E.Houseman: Last Poems

(i)

When the war ended, Clara and Marion came home. Emily had not left Glanton since the closing of Callaly hospital, and it was not long before Florence decided that she had had enough of the City where she had worked for twenty-five years. Jack was demobilized and, being the only uncommitted male, felt it his duty to stay with his mother as a long as she lived. Once again he took over the garden, assisted by a bearded gentleman called Harris who had looked after it during the war. Harris was a great character, fond of high-sounding words and quaint phrases. He was devoted to all the family, and was delighted to see us in turn when we went to Glanton in the summer – or, as he put it, 'to see all of you in rotation.' To my aunts this conjured up a picture of a bevy of Robertsons performing gyratory antics on the lawn. On one occasion he told Elizabeth that he had made a tree safe from 'mauraiders' (shades of Lewis Carroll!) Once he caught an 'imposter' in a trap, and he was proud of the 'eating propensities' of his potatoes. When he heard that Clara, just demobilized, had had a good journey, he said he was glad and 'hoped it would continue.'

The family were as fond of Harris as he of them. In 1918 and 1919, when the terrible epidemic of Spanish influenza swept the country, Glanton did not escape and Harris was one of the victims.

> *'Our poor old friend Harris is very ill,'* Elizabeth told Clara. *'I fear he will not recover ... he is delirious and very weak ...Nearly every house has an invalid ... There is not a washerwoman to be got.'*

Harris died in March, 1919, and his passing caused great grief to all the Robertsons.

> *'Our dear old friend Harris has passed away,'* Emily told Clara.

151

'Tim, I loved that dear old man, and feel just as if one of our own had gone … I feel just heart broken about him.'

Harris's daughter, in her widowhood, came to live in a cottage opposite Glanton House, and proved a true friend to my aunts in their later years. Though only a few years younger than they, she spent hours in the summer picking fruit, and in the winter, too, she was in and out helping them with the more unpleasant chores. She lived to a ripe old age, dying in her nineties in 1969.

Conrad and Gertrude

Gradually life returned to normal, and in the uneasy years after the war Glanton was a haven of peace and plenty to which those of us living in cities returned thankfully every year. It often happened that Conrad and his wife, with their baby son, and my parents and I were all there at the same time. With Elizabeth, five aunts and Jack, there would be thirteen people in the house. How we were all accommodated I cannot think, but there was never any question of staggering our visits. Nothing gave Elizabeth greater pleasure than to have the whole family round her, and the three summers after the end of the war, with all her surviving children at Glanton together, were probably the happiest times she had enjoyed since William's death.

She was as busy as ever with her knitting and needlework, and must have enjoyed extraordinary good eyesight. In 1920, when a sale of work was drawing near, she wrote to Ina:

'I am nearly finished my contribution. I just have the button holes for slotting to do in the blue chemise. The embroidery looks pretty upon it, but oh dear! The button holing round the edge to top and sleeves and 68 button holes for the ribbon slotting.'

What wonderful garments we women wore fifty years ago!

There was a timeless quality about Elizabeth. To me she had always seemed an old lady, in her black dress and lace cap, but she never appeared to grow any older, and Glanton without her was unthinkable. But early in 1922 she became seriously ill, and in March of that year she died, with all the family at her bedside. For sixty-two years Elizabeth had been the chatelaine of Glanton House, the guiding light of all her children, and a dearly loved grandmother. After her death my father wrote to me, 'A light has gone out of my life for ever.' Glanton House would never be quite the same again.

Jack

(ii)

A year after Elizabeth's death, Jack went back to New Zealand and, with a legacy from his mother, bought a lemon farm at Glenfield, now a suburb of Auckland. 'Glanton without her was more than I could stand,' he wrote a year later. 'There was always the prospect of her welcome to the returned wanderer, which can never beckon any more.' He had just had a letter from his five-year-old nephew, which caused him considerable amusement:

'It ran thus: "There is a rabbit in the garden." Stupendous news in 7 words: the most expert condenser of cable messages could not beat that.'

153

It would seem from his letters that Jack was happier and more settled at Glenfield than at any time previously, and more successful. Although living on his own, he had close friends at Auckland, a Mr. and Mrs. Holmes, who welcomed him at any time and regarded him as one of the family. Whenever he felt the need of companionship and rest from his labours, he spent a few days with them and came back refreshed. He was only five miles from the small town of Albany, and he had good neighbours in Glenfield, too, where social life was not lacking. Although sixty years of age he still played tennis and enjoyed an occasional dance.

In addition to lemons he grew persimmons, loquats, apples and oats for marketing, and all kinds of vegetables for sale and for home consumption. The farm had been badly neglected, and it took him two or three years to put it in order, but it was work he enjoyed and it proved rewarding. He did not make a fortune, but his income was more than ample for his simple needs, and allowed him a few of the little luxuries he had never before been able to afford. For the first time in his life he was content.

He was interested, too, in the wildlife of New Zealand.

> 'You never saw such a country for spiders. They spin their webs everywhere, and with incredible speed and dauntless perseverance. You need never be surprised, on waking in the morning, to find your nose connected with the bedpost by a thread of gossamer ... In summer the "mason bee" is their great enemy. He catches a spider, seals it up in one of his cells, along with a bee-that-is-to-be, which young hopeful feeds on the said spider. The Mason will build several such cells, in tubular form, on your mackintosh or in the folds of any garment hanging up, also in a keyhole or convenient corner anywhere. He is a busy worker and under no trade union restrictions as to hours or speed of working. I think many of our so called labour men might learn a useful lesson from the bee.'

Will was as keen an entomologist as he had been in the old days when he chased butterflies in Epping forest, and Jack had sent him several specimens of New Zealand insects.

> 'I wish I could send Will a specimen of the mason bee's

154

workmanship,' he wrote, 'but it is not easy to send a keyhole by post, and mackintoshes are too expensive to be cut up, even if the delicate masonry would stand the trip.'

The following year, however, he did send Will a mason bee's nest, and it arrived in perfect condition. For ten years Jack's letters continued to tell of his full and happy days, his enjoyment of the New Zealand climate, his delight in his fruit and vegetable and flowers.

'Pottering about in my little cabbage patch, and sometimes long days in the orchard, keep me occupied – and happy. There is nothing like work, if congenial, for bringing a quiet content.'

But in 1935 he became very ill. For some time he had had minor heart trouble, and now his doctor told him that he must give up manual work entirely. To one of his temperament this was a shattering blow, but he found a man to do the heavy work and live in the house, and, after a month's complete rest, was so much better that he hoped to be able to return to a fairly normal, if restricted, life. But it was not to be, and he died only a few months later.

It is good to know that, after all his restless wandering, he had, at the end of his life, found happiness and peace of mind.

(iii)

After Jack's departure it was little Florence, the woman who had spent all her working life in London, who took over responsibility for the garden. It was more than a full-time job, and, although she worked from morning to night, it was beyond the capacity of any one person to keep abreast of it. But, though the weeds flourished and the flower beds were no longer as immaculate as before, it was seldom that the household lacked fruit and vegetables. Florence did a magnificent job. But, in spite of her valiant efforts, nature gradually took over. Every year, when we went to Glanton, a little more of the garden had gone back to the wild. The tennis court, unused now, had again become part of the croft. The old apple trees bore little fruit, and the paths were grass grown.

With rising costs, the five women found their meagre income barely sufficient, even for their simple needs. The house was too big for them, and little was done to keep it in order. 'It will last our time,' they said. As in most old houses, the water tanks were in the garret and, the Northumbrian climate being what it is, it was seldom that a winter passed without burst pipes. The tanks were over the guest room, and year after year the water would pour through the ceiling on to the treasured feather bed and into the drawing-room underneath. The mattress had to be dragged downstairs and draped over a clothes horse to dry in front of the kitchen fire – an operation that might take weeks. Sometimes to provide a little variety, it would be the pipes in the lavatory halfway up the stairs that burst, sending a cascade of water down the stairs and flooding hall and kitchen. Fortunately there was a kindly plumber in the village, and a number of obliging neighbours to help with the mopping-up operations. But, in spite of all the drawbacks, they never for a moment considered leaving their beloved home; it would have broken their hearts.

Twice a day, a small child fetched milk from a farm, for which she received sixpence a week. Bottles did not appear in Glanton until about the time of the Second World War, and the milk was brought in cans, more or less straight from the cow. It seemed to us town-dwellers unnecessary to have the milk fetched twice in one day, but to my aunts it would have been unthinkable not to have 'new milk' in the evening. Though they might, with apologies, use up the morning's milk in our coffee at supper-time, they would never give it to the cats. They maintained that the cats would not drink milk that was not fresh.

Animals played a large part in the life at Glanton House. After William's death there were no more ponies, but there was generally a dog, and always at least one cat. The first dog I remember was a curly-haired black retriever called Oscar, who generally occupied the best armchair, and he was followed by Nigger, another black retriever. They belonged to Clara. But the dog I remember best is Paddy, a beautiful but completely undisciplined red setter. Officially he belonged to Florence, who claimed that he was absolutely obedient. If we took Paddy for a romp on Glanton Hill, he would immediately race away out of sight on his own urgent business (which, as often as not, was chasing sheep). When it was time to go home, Florence would summon him with a shrill blast on a police-type whistle. Nothing happened. 'He'll soon come,' she would say optimistically. Every few minutes she would repeat the ear-splitting blast, which must have been audible half a mile away. Perhaps twenty minutes later his business completed, Paddy would amble back, wagging his tail. 'Isn't he a good dog?' Florence would say. 'He always comes to the whistle.' Well, maybe – in his own good time.

The first cat in my Glanton life was Ching, the Siamese, who unlike most of his race, was enormously fat. He was a very dignified and well-behaved cat. Any food left lying about within his reach was quite safe; it would have been beneath his Siamese dignity to descend to larceny. Only once did he err in this respect. When I was a very small child he brought in a baby rabbit. 'We'll keep that for Joyce's dinner,' said my fond grandmother. She skinned it, cut it up, and put the pieces in a bowl of water in the pantry. But when, a little later, she went to fetch it, the rabbit had disappeared, though not a drop of water had been spilled. Through the window she saw my lord Ching in the yard, happily eating Joyce's dinner. And who would blame him? He had, after all, caught the rabbit; he had every moral right to it.

There followed a succession of cats, mostly of the marmalade variety, each one fatter than the last. They would not eat fish or any ordinary meat – only rabbit or liver – and refused milk that was not absolutely fresh. Emily had many an argument with the village butcher, who did not share her passion for cats, or indeed for any members of the animal kingdom. ('I don't believe in birds,' he once said). Sometimes Emily would make a special journey to Alnwick by bus to procure the right kind of meat for Simba or Freckles or Winston or Tuppenny, whoever the current cat might be.

Elizabeth kept hens for many years and, though they lived in the dovecote, they were almost members of the family. An ailing hen would be tenderly laid on a blanket in front of the kitchen fire. A friend once suggested that they should keep a pig, but they thought it would be rather difficult. 'You see,' said Emily, 'we'd soon get so fond of it, we'd have it lying on the hearth rug with the cats – and it would be rather big, don't you think?'

Every year my aunts received a letter from some authority thanking them for their past co-operation in shooting rooks, and asking for their continued help. This went straight into the fire. Shoot rooks indeed!

They had never had a rook shot in their lives, and never would.

A series of village maidens came to help in the house, most of whom seemed to be called Violet ('Vi'let' in local parlance). They were, as a rule, very young, and some of them did not appear to be particularly efficient, but any pair of hands was better than none, for apart from Marion all the aunts loathed house work – most of all Emily, who had changed greatly from the busy little housewife of seventeen who had managed so well and with such pride in the 1880s when Elizabeth was in London. At one time the 'help' was a woman of more mature years, a lady of great dignity, little conversation and no sense of humour. She had three daughters, to whom she referred as 'th'alder yin, the middle yin and the ti'ither yin.' She arrived early every morning, Sundays included and was given her breakfast. One Sunday Emily said, 'We have a treat this morning – kippers.' The 'help' drew herself up to her full height, looked down her long nose and said, 'I've niver aten a kipper on a Sunday in a' me life, and I'm no startin' the noo.' Emily, snubbed and speechless, crept guiltily away to eat her sacrilegious kipper in the dining-room.

The five sisters would have been content to spend the rest of their lives quietly at Glanton House, but prices continued to rise and, however economical they were, they found it difficult to make ends meet, so soon after Elizabeth's death Marion took a post as housekeeper to a young widower at Chapel-en-le-Frith. She stayed there for several years, until his children went to school. Ina, after leaving the hospital at Dunstan-on-Tyne, taught a little boy at Newton Stewart. It was not until shortly before the Second World War that the sisters were again united at Glanton. They were by then all in their sixties and seventies, and lived out the rest of their lives in honourable retirement.

The years passed, and there was little change in their way of life. Very occasionally one of them would visit us in London, but for the most part they were quite content to stay in their own home. Though they lived in such a backwater, they kept well up with current trends. During the long winter evenings they were great readers, and could discuss intelligently all the latest books, and even the plays that were running in London, though it was very seldom that they visited the theatre. They were to the fore in all village activities, regularly attending the Women's Institute and choir practice, and taking a stall at every sale of work. Emily took a correspondence course in Greek when she was in her eighties and wrote quite charming poetry. In fact they lived very full lives.

(iv)

For me the years between the wars were a period of great change. After graduating from St. Hugh's College, Oxford, I spent three years in the Education Department of the British Broadcasting Company, as it then was. This was in the old days of '2LO' at Savoy Hill. Broadcasting was in its infancy, everyone knew everyone else, and there was an almost happy-go-lucky atmosphere. I was once given the opportunity to witness one of the early experiments in television, then a dream of the future. Though it was only a small picture of a soprano at full blast, it seemed little short of a miracle – and it was in colour.

It was at about this time that I had a very uncanny experience during a holiday at Glanton. My father had driven a car-load to our favourite picnic spot among the Cheviots beside the little river Breamish, and I and another member of the party climbed a small hill to get up an appetite for tea. At the top we found a long, flat rock and sat down to rest. Everything was peaceful and beautiful, the silence broken only by the distant bleating of sheep and the happy voices of our friends preparing tea at the foot of the hill. The sun was shining, and the hills had never looked more bonny. Yet suddenly my flesh began to creep, and I felt myself surrounded by something so eerie and malignant that, to the surprise of my companion, I jumped to my feet and ran down that hillside as if the devil himself were after me – and indeed I felt that he was. My friend followed at a more leisurely pace. 'Why on earth did you run away like that?' he asked. I could not explain. There is nothing sinister about those gentle green hills, which I had known and loved all my life. I only knew that I felt hemmed in by something so overpoweringly evil that I could not have stayed another minute on that rock. Later, a possible explanation occurred to me. On the opposite hill across the valley are the remains of an ancient British camp. Could it be that that innocuous-looking rock on which we had been sitting had once been a sacrificial stone?

YEARS OF CHANGE

'Goodbye, Piccadilly, Farewell Leicester Squre'
It's a long way to Tipperary

(i)

In 1937 Will, who was seventy four, decided to retire and to move out of London, which we all disliked. In the autumn of that year I took a job at the Radcliffe Infirmary in Oxford and, for the first few months, lived in a bed-sitting room in St John Street. By a strange coincidence my landlady was a Northumbrian from Wooler. My fellow lodgers were members of the Playhouse Company. The Playhouse in Beaumont Street was new since my college days; the original repertory company had played at the 'Red Barn' in Woodstock Road when two almost unknown young actors, John and Val Gielgud, were pin-up boys of the women under-graduates.

In January 1938, we moved into a house in Summertown. It had a small garden, and Will did not relish the prospect of coping with it. He had done no gardening since his young days at Glanton House and had no wish to start again in his old age. Our London house had had a small space at the back which called itself a garden but, owing to poor soil, an underground river and various other impediments, nothing would grow in it. Even an attempt to cultivate grounsel for the canary was a lamentable failure and our only successful crop ever was some artichokes that flourished, more or less, during the First World War. Yet after a few months in Oxford, Will had become as ardent a gardener as his sister Florence. Small though the garden was, he kept us supplied with vegetables all through the year and even found room for a tiny strawberry bed and a few bushes of soft fruit. So it was that the two London exiles became the most enthusiastic and successful horticulturists.

Delighted at having escaped from the noise and bustle of London, we all looked forward to a few years of happiness in our new home, but the peace did not last. After only a few months came the Munich crisis and a year later the outbreak of the Second World War. Although he had officially retired, Will did not wish to give up medical work entirely and during our first two summers in Oxford he went to London several times as locum for some of his doctor friends. When war broke out he immediately enrolled in the Emergency Medical Service and answered many calls from the Oxfordshire Division. At first he still gave preference to his London friends in the summer, but when the blitz started in earnest Dora begged him not to go to London. Reluctantly he agreed, but when the air raids seemed to have eased off he once again deputised for an old friend in Woolwich. As luck would have it, it was while he was there that the first V.1s arrived and Dora was frantic with worry but Will was quite unmoved.

In October 1944 however, he became seriously ill and was admitted to the Radcliffe Infirmary for an operation for cancer. In spite of his eighty one years he made a marvellous recovery and endeared himself to the doctors and nurses by his patience and lack of complaint. The only complaint he did make was when he, a north countryman, was given sugar in his porridge. Within a remarkably short time he was as fit as ever and back to work in his beloved garden. In the spring he once again took up work under the Emergency Service.

(ii)

Will had given up his car when we left London. I had hoped to run one myself but the war put an end to my hopes for several years and once more our visits to Glanton were made by train. It took us back to the old days before the First World War, except that Foggin and his wagonette had long since departed this life, and we were now met by a taxi.

At Glanton House there was at first little change. My aunts were amazed to hear that our milk was rationed and that we were allowed only one egg per person per week. They were, of course, too old for active war work but all through the war they looked after a succession of small girls, evacuees from Tyneside. They were all devoted to children, and the little girls entrusted to their care were very fortunate. There were two of whom they became particularly fond. On the first Sunday after these two arrived Lorna, the younger, was making very heavy weather of her dinner. 'Why aren't you eating, hinny?' asked Emily, 'Don't you like it?' Lorna gave a big sigh. 'Oh ay,' she replied, 'but I wuddn't mind a moog o'beeor the day.' This was, apparently, the normal Sunday drink for a six year old in the Tyneside home.

Since his retirement, Will had taken his part in the household chores and always helped with the washing up, an occupation he quite enjoyed. 'I can't think why people dislike it so much,' he often said. But in the Victorian atmosphere of Glanton House it was unheard of for the man of the house to perform such menial chores, and when the meal was over Will was firmly pushed into the best armchair while the rest of us retired to the kitchen. Will resented this. 'I may be old,' he said, 'but I'm not too decrepit to wash up.' But his protests went unheeded until one day someone heard that he really <u>liked</u> washing up. After that, not only was he allowed to help but, if for some reason he forgot and disappeared when the meal was finished, no one was allowed to begin until he came back. 'Will likes to do it, so we must wait for him,' they said. The man of the house must always be indulged, and we women must wait upon his pleasure.

And a man could do no wrong. Among the aunts' acquaintances were a married couple who had separated, each having a mild, and possibly harmless, <u>affaire</u> with someone else. The wife became ' that dreadful woman' whose 'disgraceful behaviour' shocked them to the core; but her husband's lapse was described as 'a beautiful little idyll.'

(iii)

When the war ended in September 1945, Will and Dora hoped that at last they would be able to enjoy a few years of happiness in their retirement; but it was short lived. In the autumn Dora was found to have cancer. She came through the operation well, and in early December Will took her to Chipping Campden to recuperate. Although the war was over food and drink were still in very short supply, and she wrote to me, 'Dad managed to get Guinness for me, which I enjoyed... The barman told him he can only serve 3 glasses per day.' I was joining them for the weekend, and Dora asked me to bring her a box of matches, as she was not sure she could get any in Chipping Campden. She also mentioned that a chicken was being posted to us all the way from Glanton, as otherwise we would probably have had no bird for Christmas.

Unfortunately Dora's operation had come too late. By the end of January she was again very ill, and was not expected to live for more than six months at most. I was working long hours at the hospital and it was impossible for me to look after her so, in desperation, I asked Marion if she would come to us for a short time until we could make other arrangements. She arrived two days later, prepared to stay for as long as she was needed. I realised then, as never before, what a wonderful person she was. Not only was she a first class nurse, but she insisted on taking over the running of the house and most of the cooking, ever patient, ever sweet-tempered and cheerful. She was in her seventies and I felt that she was shouldering too great a burden but when I suggested that Dora should go to a nursing home she would hear none of it. 'I will stay until the end,' she said, and she did.

Dora died in May 1946. No-one could have wanted her illness prolonged, but her death left a great blank in our lives. She and I had been very close companions and I missed her sadly. It was probably even worse for Will, for I was out all day and he led rather a lonely life but, as I was the breadwinner, it was impossible for me to give up my job. He had, however, become very domesticated, coped with the shopping, prepared vegetables, and did everything possible to make things easier for me. Apart from losing weight he showed no ill-effects of his illness, worked hard in the garden and spent several weeks in London every summer as locum.

It was while he was deputising for his old friend in Clapham in September 1948 that he again became very ill. I fetched him home and a few weeks later he was admitted to the Radcliffe Infirmary. I sent a telegram to Glanton and Emily arrived next day to be near the brother who, of all the family, had been closest to her and most beloved. Once in hospital, Will seemed to lose the will to live, and he died only four days later.

After his death I had a charming letter from the secretary of the Oxfordshire Division Medical Committee:

'I wish to pay tribute to his memory,' he wrote. 'At an age when he might quite honourably have sought retirement and rest from a strenuous career, he became a most useful and _active_ member of the Oxford Medical Profession... He has indeed served his *generation well and nobly, and has deserved, and has, our unbounded gratitude.'*

But perhaps the tribute I appreciated most was a brief note from one of the London doctors for whom Will had often acted as locum:

'So the grand old man has gone. We were very fond of him. We shall miss him. We shall not see his like again.'

And I myself could truly echo Will's own words when <u>his</u> father died: 'Rarely have any children had so dear and good a father.'

(iv)

Though born and bred in London I had always been a countrywoman at heart and after my father's death I moved to a cottage in North Oxfordshire. Here several of my aunts visited me in turn (or, as Harris would have said, 'in rotation'). The first to come was Florence, who spent a week with me in the summer of 1950. The following year she and Emily went for a rare holiday to the Isle of Arran – 'the epitome of Scotland' as Emily described it. But the day after their arrival Florence became very ill and Emily brought her straight back to Glanton. She was, in fact, suffering from pneumonia, and a fortnight later she died.

Joyce with some of her Aunts circa 1950s

To her sisters this probably caused a greater sense of loss than even the death of their brothers. Jack and Alfred had both been abroad for many years when they died, and Conrad (who had died in 1940) and Will had visited Glanton only in the summer, but for nearly twenty years the five sisters had lived together at Glanton House and Florence's empty place was a sad reminder that they were all getting old and that the little family might soon be further reduced. It was, in fact, only two years before Clara followed Florence, and before the end of 1955 Marion, too, was dead.

Now only Emily and Ina were left – the eldest and the youngest of the sisters. Though they were devoted to each other, they had not a great deal in common. Emily was now in her ninetieth year but her brilliant brain was in no way impaired and Ina, always the least intellectual of the family and by now beginning to show signs of the mental deterioration which overtook her later, was all too conscious of her inability to provide her eldest sister with the mental stimulus she needed. She was also inclined to resent Emily's domination. 'There's no need to treat me as a child,' she once complained to me, 'just because Em is ninety and I'm only eighty.' Now these two were left on their own, and each in her own way was lonely; Ina bereft without her beloved Marion and Emily missing the soothing presence of the gentle Clara, the nearest to her in age.

Emily, at ninety one, was as hale and hearty as ever and there seemed to be no reason why she should not live to be a hundred. But one day she slipped on the post office steps and fractured her femur. 'How silly of me!' was all she said when she was picked up. She was taken to Alnwick Infirmary and, when I visited her a week or two later, I hardly recognised her. The gay vital active woman I had known was now just a little wizened old lady, and I knew that even her indomitable spirit could not save her. She died in January 1958, within three months of her ninety second birthday.

I went to Glanton for a long weekend to attend the funeral and cope with the most urgent affairs. In her bedroom there was an old fashioned wash-stand with a marble top, and the usual Victorian china jug and basin, slop bucket etc., – and the bucket was full of pound notes. I forget how much money there was – subsequent events made me lose count of it – but the bucket was full to the brim. And that was only the beginning.

Wherever I went I found money – in books, under a cupboard, tucked away among Emily's clothes – several hundred pounds in all. How she accumulated so much was, and still is, a mystery. She and her sisters had always appeared to be hard up and, though generous to others, were reluctant to spend a penny on themselves or on the house. Yet here were hundreds of pounds lying around collected, it would seem, by Emily, since Ina denied all knowledge of the money. It must have taken her years to save so much from her small income. And why had she not paid the money into the bank?

But the strangest find was in the black tin box in which they kept important documents and their respective contributions to the housekeeping purse. Here I found three bundles of new notes, a hundred pounds in each, still fastened in paper bands as drawn from the bank. But why? One possible explanation occurred to me. Every Christmas the sisters sent quite large donations to their pet charities and, knowing their little ways, I can well believe that instead of writing cheques they may have sent their gifts in treasury notes by registered post. It was shortly before Christmas that Emily's accident occurred, and possibly she had just drawn out three hundred pounds but had not had time to send it to the charities. But why, with so much already in the house, should she have drawn out more? Was she saving up for something special? We shall never know.

One thing was clear; I could not leave hundreds of pounds in the house, nor did I fancy carrying all those notes by train to Oxfordshire. But the nearest bank was in Alnwick, I had no car, and there was no time to go by bus, for I was going home on that night's train. The kind friend next door came to my rescue. She lent me her car and I drove to Alnwick and thankfully paid the money into Ina's account. It took a great weight off my mind. Now I could spend the few remaining hours in tidying up Emily's affairs.

Or so I thought. But I had not been back in the house half an hour before I found yet another hoard – a mere eighty pounds this time, and again all in pound notes. This was the last straw. It is not often that one is sorry to find money, but I had reached the point of feeling that if I came across one more pound note in that house I should go round the bend. And what was I to do with eighty pounds? Ina was about to go to her nephew's house in Hampshire, and Glanton House would be empty.

166

There was only one solution – to ask the friend next door to take charge of the money and pay it into Ina's account in due course. But this had to be done in great secrecy. One of Ina's idiosyncrasies was a belief that her neighbours – and indeed all the village – were trying to pry into her affairs. 'Whenever they come into the house,' she said, 'they peer all round to see what they can see. They're all inquisitive.' There was, of course, no foundation for Ina's suspicions; it was merely the imagining of her confused mind. But I tremble to think what she would have said had she known I was entrusting her money to someone else! So, feeling like a conspirator, I crept round to the house next door and handed over the last of the cash.

CHAPTER XI

JUST INA

'Last of that bright band'
Felicia Hemans: The Graves of a Household

(i)

Poor little Ina! Of all the sisters she was the least fitted to be left on her own. Owing to her 'youth' she had never been allowed to make any decisions in domestic matters and had always been shielded from unpleasantness by her elder sisters. (During Marion's last illness, it was not until near the end that Emily let her be told that her favourite sister was dying, because she did not want to upset her.) She had not an inkling as to her financial position and was quite incapable of coping with household matters. She had even forgotten how to cook. Emily's death left her utterly bewildered and helpless and aggravated the deterioration in her mental condition. From being considered a child she now became childish. Though overwhelmed with grief by the loss of her sister, she yet took a pathetic pleasure in her newly acquired status as mistress of Glanton House. 'I am "Miss Robertson" now,' she said proudly. No longer 'Miss Ina' but 'Miss Robertson'. The trouble was that she was not capable of living up to her new responsibilities.

It was obvious that she could not live alone but at first she firmly refused to have a resident housekeeper. Eventually, however, she agreed to consider the matter and the next question was which of the now unoccupied bedrooms should be turned into a sitting room for the housekeeper. To Ina there was no problem at all. 'She can sit in the kitchen' she said. It had to be explained to her that, unlike the daily maid, Hannah, in the old days, housekeepers did not sit in kitchens.

The next problem was to find a suitable person for the post and this, we knew, might be difficult. Glanton House, for all its charms, was not the height of comfort. With its clutter of old-fashioned furniture and bric-a-brac, it was not an easy house to run; there were no modern appliances, no comfortable beds and, in the winter, it was like an ice-house. It also had to be admitted that poor little Ina, in her present confused state, would not be too easy to live with. But it was Ina herself who eventually

Miss L. Robertson

to

Exors. of H. W. T. Mason deceased.

Rent due					
1962.	To Half-Year's Rent of				
Nov. 11	Mansion House		£	20	-

Paid

2 6 NOV 1962

Property Tax ....

One of the last rent receipts honouring a century old agreement

solved the problem for us; she dug in her toes and said that she would have no stranger in the house. There was only one person, and one only, whom she would consider. This was a woman who lived in the village and had for many years given occasional help with the housework. She was approached and, mercifully, agreed to come. She knew Ina and her funny little ways and was endowed with considerable patience and she stayed at her post as long as Ina remained at Glanton House.

For several years Ina muddled along, growing more and more confused and frail until, in 1963, she became really ill and was admitted to a hospital in North Shields. It was clear that she could never go back to Glanton House so, when the hospital had done all they could for her, she went to a home in Whitley Bay. She was not told that she could not return to her own home, nor would she have understood, for by this time her mind was hopelessly confused. She lived in the past, sometimes believing that her eldest brother Will, who had not lived there since 1881, was still at Glanton House. Once she told me that she was at the Home to help the nurses, harking back to her nursing days in the First World War, probably the happiest years of her life. When I visited her she was always pleased to see me, though she had no idea who I was. Yet she was quite content in her own little private world. Early in 1965 she contracted bronchitis and died on 16th February in her ninetieth year. It was almost exactly 106 years since the young Elizabeth had first come to Glanton – on St Valentine's Day 1859.

(ii)

When, in 1963, it had become apparent that Ina could never return to Glanton, there loomed the appalling task of clearing out the house. The family had been in occupation for more that a hundred years and no one, it seemed, had ever thrown anything away. It was a daunting prospect and I was reminded of a remark Emily had made to me some years earlier. 'I'm sorry for you when you have to clear this place out,' she said, 'I suggest you just blow it up.' Now the time had come and I was inclined to agree with her! Both I and my co-executor, whom I will call Henry, were working for our respective livings, and Glanton was three hundred miles away. We did not relish the thought of spending the whole of our precious summer holidays on house-clearance, and Henry had a bright idea. 'Let's go up for alternate weekends during the summer,' he suggested. I did not greatly care for the idea; rushing to London straight

170

from the office on Friday evening, travelling up to Alnwick on the night train, slogging all the weekend, back on the Sunday night train and straight to the office on Monday morning. I am not as young as I was. However, to show willing, I agreed to try it and one weekend in May we made the long, tedious journey arriving at Glanton House in time for breakfast, which Ina's former housekeeper had laid on for us.

Thus fortified, we prepared to set to. 'Where shall we start?' asked Henry. I looked round rather helplessly. 'Well, since we're in the dining room, let's start here,' I suggested, stifling a yawn. We turned out one cupboard crammed with letters, address books, unintelligible memoranda and a motley collection of odds and ends but, after throwing out a few bits of obvious rubbish, we weakly put the rest back. We were not feeling at our brightest and best. Hopefully, we opened the cellarette but found, to our disappointment, that it contained only ginger wine and lemonade – and one bottle of brandy, thick with dust and nearly empty. 'That won't be any good,' sighed Henry but I sniffed it, gulped down the little that remained, and felt much better. Then we turned our attention to a large built-in cupboard beside the fireplace. Here we found box upon box of biscuits and sweets, obviously given to the aunts as Christmas presents and never opened (some I recognised as my own gifts of years gone by). Unfortunately, they had all been hoarded so long that most of them were inedible.

All day we ploughed through cupboards and drawers but when, in the evening, we surveyed the result of our efforts, it did not seem to amount to much. 'Ah well, there's still tomorrow,' we sighed as we yawned our way to bed. But when Sunday came we felt far from energetic. We were visiting Ina in the afternoon so there was not much time anyway; it hardly seemed worthwhile starting. We pottered about, doing this and that, but by lunchtime there was little to show for our labours. After visiting Ina, we dined in Newcastle and were then faced with another night journey. To crown it all, there were no sleepers available in the second class carriages. The thought of sitting up all night was more that we could bear, so we changed to first class and travelled to King's Cross in comparative comfort. 'I don't think we'll do this again,' said Henry. 'No,' I agreed. We didn't.

But the house had to be cleared somehow and now there was a deadline.

By a coincidence the landlord had decided to sell all his Glanton property the following autumn, and naturally would like Glanton House with vacant possession. During the summer I went back to Glanton, with a friend to help, and the following day Henry arrived, accompanied by his wife and seventeen year old son. We had just a fortnight to complete the job. Even with five pairs of hands it took a long, long time to wade through the ground floor rooms, the cellar and the bedrooms, and we were frequently sidetracked by finding treasures – a complete Copeland dinner service, beautiful needlework of a bygone age, a chest of lovely Irish silver. All had been hidden away for untold years and even I, who had known Glanton House all my life, had no idea that they existed. Then there were all the out-buildings – dovecote, stables, saddle-room, granary. And the great mangle. What on earth were we to do with that? We did try to get rid of it. We offered it to museums but they were not interested. In the end, I regret to say, we left it for the next owners. I hope they appreciated it.

But the real nightmare was the garret which we left until the end knowing what a ghastly task it would be. Only one of the three rooms had electric light and in the other two, with their sloping roofs and tiny cobwebbed windows, we groped our way in semi-darkness as we turned out box after box, trunk after trunk, chest of drawers after chest of drawers. And what a heterogeneous collection of stuff it was! In one trunk we found yards and yards of beautiful new material, evidently bought by the sisters for their handiwork and never used, while in another hardby were clothes of the mid-Victorian era, probably part of Elizabeth's trousseau from over a century before – a pair of white kid boots, a white feather muff, charming little bonnets, a lovely frilly white dress which may have been her wedding gown. One of William's long nightshirts was there too, and his night-cap with its little tassel. There were cases of old letters, without which this story could not have been written. There was Jack's old Mountie uniform. There were flags of all nations, false teeth, old corsets. And there were six charming samplers, the oldest worked in 1805 by Ann Bolton (younger sister of Jane, who married the Rev. James of Wooler), the most recent the work of the ten year old Clara. Hanging on the walls were rows of baskets, mostly full of worn, rusty pots and pans and kettles. On a shelf we found jars of pickled snakes and other creatures, perhaps relics of Will's childhood, and some revolting cloth-covered basins which, on being opened, were found to contain the mouldy and disintegrating remains of ancient Christmas puddings. The list could go on forever; 'you name it, we have it.' Gradually, we sorted the chaff from the wheat. The seventeen year old was put in charge of 'Operation Bonfire' and, day after day, the beacon burned. We picked out the least battered of the trunks and crammed them with books, photographs, letters and other paraphernalia to be sent to our respective homes for sorting out at leisure.

Some villagers gladly relieved us of old carpets, cushions, table cloths – anything that was portable. A silversmith came from Newcastle, an antique dealer from Kendal. Jack's uniform and some of the period clothes I gave to the village dramatic society, but I had not the heart to hand over Elizabeth's pretty white dress and her muff and kid boots. Yet if I took them home I should merely transfer them from one attic to another. I had no children to inherit them and they would eventually rot away or be consigned to the dustbin. But the antique dealer was on the committee of his local museum; he was delighted to accept them and I knew that they would be carefully preserved. He took some of Elizabeth's bonnets too, and William's night-cap with its perky little tassel. He tried it on, looked at himself in the mirror and said, 'Won't my wife get a shock when I go to bed tonight?'

When the house was emptied of everything but the furniture that was to go to the local sale-room, we locked the door for the last time and heaved a great sigh of relief. The seemingly impossible task had been completed and, our consciences clear, Henry and his family went home while I went off to spend the remainder of my holiday in the blissful peace of the Outer Hebrides.

But relief was mixed with sadness. It was hard to say goodbye to the old house where I had spent so many happy holidays, hard to realise that, after more than a century, it would pass into alien hands, that never again would it be my second home, with its warm welcome and the cheerful presence of the dear aunts. But, though 'the Robertsons of Glanton' have gone forever, I like to think that their valiant spirits still linger within those walls, and that they have left behind them some sense of the graciousness and happiness of days gone by, to warm the hearts of those who come after them.

Middle Barton,
Oxfordshire.
February, 1975

ADDENDUM

Donald Robertson's Concerns

I came across correspondence referring to Singin' Hinnies after Donald (my stepfather) died in 2002. Donald had felt that the Aunts would come across as "church mice" in any family history and he had become reluctant to contribute to the project at all. He insisted that his name (where mentioned in the closing pages) should be changed – and it was. He became "Henry" whilst my mother and I remain anonymous. However when he saw the finished document he realised that his fears were unfounded and tried (too late) to have his real name reinstated. A pity perhaps, but this gives me the opportunity to set the record straight and put an identity to this mysterious newcomer!

Mervyn Cully
31st March 2010

Robertson Family Bible

Family Register

William Robertson, of Glanton – County Northumberland, and Elizabeth Ann White of Sunderland – county of Durham – were married at St. Thomas' Church, Bishopwearmouth on the 20th day of September – 1860

Their Children.

1. William Robertson, Born at Glanton, Northumberland on Sunday, the 23rd June 1861, at 5 o'clock in the evening – Died about 10 o'clock same day

2. William John Robertson. Born at Glanton Sunday the 24th May 1863 at ½ past 5 o'clock in the evening –
Baptized by Revd David Fotheringham, Presbyterian Minister of Glanton 26th June 1863.

3. John Robertson – Born at Glanton. on Friday the 14th October 1864, at a few minutes past 1 o'clock in the morning – wearmouth Baptized by Revd David Fotheringham on the 2nd December 1864

Robertson Family Bible

4. Elizabeth Emily Robertson. Born at Glanton on Tuesday the 3rd April 1866 at half past 1 o'clock in the morning – Baptized by Revd. R. H. Davidson – Presbyterian Minister of Glanton on the 29th June 1866

5. James Robertson – Born at Glanton on Thursday the 20th September 1867 at ¼ past 10 o'clock in the morning – Died at 20 minutes to 12 o'clock same evening

6. Clara Jane Robertson – Born at Glanton on Thursday the 13th October 1870 at ½ past 5 o'clock in the evening. Baptized by Revd. R. H. Davidson 15th December 1870

7. Florence Robertson – Born at Glanton on Sunday the 10th March 1872 at 20 minutes to 4 o'clock in the afternoon. Baptized by Revd. R. H. Davidson 5th April 1872

8. Marion Robertson. Born at Glanton on Tuesday the 2nd September 1873 at ½ past 9 o'clock in the morning. Baptized by Revd. R. H. Davidson – on the 14th October 1873

9. Lavinia Robertson. Born at Glanton, on Thursday the 7th October 1875 - at about 9 o'clock in the morning Baptized by Revd R. H. Davidson on the 5th November 1875

10 Alfred Edward Robertson. Born at Glanton. on Friday the 23rd March 1877 - at about half past one in the morning. Baptized by Revd R. H. Davidson on the 4th May 1877

11. Conrad James Robertson - Born at Glanton on Monday. The 13th May 1878 at about half past three in the morning Baptized by Revd R. H. Davidson on the 1st July. 1878

The family register above and on previous pages is believed to have been copied from the family Bible in an unknown hand.

Singin' Hinnies Receipe

If you don't have an open fire and a griddle, make these in a heavy frying pan on top of the stove.

Ingredients
1 lbs self-raising flour
2 ½ oz butter
2 1/2 oz lard
12 oz currants
pinch salt
2 tablespoons milk mixed with sour cream
(more if needed)
water
lard for griddle
butter for spreading

Method
Rub the fats into the flour, add salt, currants, and just enough milk and water to make a soft dough. Roll out into rounds 3/8 of an inch thick on floured surface and bake on both sides on a hot griddle until golden brown. Spread immediately with butter and cut into quarters, serving immediately.

Makes about four rounds. Double or triple the mixture depending on how many hinnies you have!